THE AGE OF APOSTOLIC APOSTLESHIP SERIES

Laying
Foundations PART 1

On Behalf of

Connecting for Excellence
International Apostolic Network

CHURCHES AND MINISTRIES IN ASSOCIATION

By Dr. Alan Pateman

By Dr. Jennifer Pateman

Available from APMI Publications, Amazon.com and Other Retail Outlets

THE AGE OF APOSTOLIC APOSTLESHIP SERIES

Laying
Foundations
PART 1

DR. ALAN PATEMAN

BOOK TITLE: Laying Foundations
(The Age of Apostolic Apostleship Series) Part One

WRITTEN BY Dr. ALAN PATEMAN
ISBN: 978-1-909132-56-6
eBook ISBN: 978-1-909132-57-3

Published By:
APMI Publications
In Partnership with Truth for the Journey Books **19**
Email: publications@alanpateman.com
www.AlanPatemanMinistries.com

Acknowledgements:
Author/Design/Senior Editor/Publisher: Apostle Dr. Alan Pateman
Editing/Proofreading/Research: Dr. Jennifer Pateman
Computer Administration/Office Manager: Dr. Dorothea Struhlik
Cover Image Credit: www.PosterMyWall.com

❖

Dedication

To all my CFE Friends.

❖

Table of Contents

❖

Acknowledgement

This book "Laying Foundations" is part of the Age of the Apostolic Apostleship Series, an update of my book "Apostles – Can the Church Survive without Them?" My intention here is to give all those who are and will become part of "Connecting for Excellence International Apostolic Network" some foundation for their ministries.

❖

Introduction

I cannot express my gratitude enough to all those who have encouraged me to establish that which you will find in this book **"Laying Foundations,"** Part One of the Age of the Apostolic Apostleship Series.

But this is not something that one wakes up to one morning and decides to begin or develop. It was not my intention to develop a network out of some response, because of a lack of associations or denominational structures, *remember there is only One Body.*

It is not because someone encouraged me to put down on paper my thoughts of how and what a network is or consists of. As you will see in my introduction, there are many wonderful and well-established organizations that I would only be too pleased to submit under and help to develop.

But God over the years, to my surprise, has led me in a direction to *help develop others in their quest to fulfil the dream* that God has placed within their heart. This began to materialize in the late 1980's, although at the time, I did not know that the word apostle existed. We were always encouraged by the pastoral gift, with the occasional glimpse of perhaps that evading evangelist.

At the beginning of the 1990's God began to speak to me prophetically through men of God, like Doctor Roberts Liardon with words of direction and encouragement, that God was raising me up in the apostolic ministry. This was apparent as time went on for I found that different ministries were coming to me for prayer, impartation, anointing and ordination.

This developed into the establishing of "Friends in Ministry" in relationship with Pastor Andy Wall, then at the advice and direction of Doctor Robb Thompson into **"Connecting for Excellence"** International Apostolic Network (2000), a multi-facetted missions organization as I have travelled widely throughout Europe, Africa, Asia and America.

Serving more than 500 ministers that I have to-date ordained in over fifty nations along with ministries, churches and schools in association or affiliation from around the globe.

I pray as you read this book "Laying Foundations" that you will find that the Holy Spirit will impart to you the vision of Apostolic Networking, and then together we can work for the glory of the Almighty God.

Apostle Alan Pateman, Ph.D., D.Min., D.D.

❖

CHAPTER 1

Passing the Baton
between Generations

Let's look in detail at recent church history in order to view how the apostolic "baton" was successfully passed from one generation to the next. Knowing that through the perseverance and obedience of others - history as we know it was altered forever! In particular we are going to look at how things progressed from the "Azusa Street Revival" onwards and how certain individual's affected their own era, while still affecting our lives today.

One generation will praise your deeds to the next. Each generation will talk about your mighty acts.

(Psalms 145:4 GW)

To begin with and in addition to the ministers who received their Pentecostal experience at Azusa Street, thousands - millions of others were indirectly influenced by the revival in Los Angeles. Among them was Thomas Ball Barratt of Norway, a Methodist pastor who became known as the Pentecostal Apostle to Northern and Western Europe.

After being baptized in the Holy Spirit and receiving tongues in New York City in 1906, Barratt returned to Oslo where, in December 1906, he conducted the first Pentecostal services in Europe. From Norway, Barratt travelled to Sweden, England, France and Germany where he sparked other national Pentecostal movements. Under Barratt, such leaders a Lewi Pethrus in Sweden, Jonathan Paul in Germany and Alexander Bobby in England were brought into the movement.

The Chicago Influence

From Chicago, through the influence of William Durham, the movement spread quickly to Italy and South America. Two Italian immigrants from Chicago, Luigi Francescon and Giacomo Lombardy founded thriving Italian Pentecostal movements after 1908 in the United States, Brazil, Argentina and Italy.

In South Bend, Indiana - near Chicago - two Swedish Baptist immigrants, Daniel Berg and Gunnar Vingren, received the Pentecostal experience. Believing they were called prophetically to Brazil, they embarked on a missionary trip in 1910 that resulted in the formation of the Brazilian Assemblies of God.

The Brazilian Assemblies developed into the largest national Pentecostal movement in the world and had some 25 million members by 1990. Also hailing from Chicago was Willis C. Hoover, the Methodist missionary to Chile who in 1909 led a Pentecostal revival in the Chilean Methodist Episcopal Church.

After being excommunicated from the Methodist Episcopal Church, Hoover and 37 of his followers organized the Pentecostal Methodist Church, which has some 1.5 million adherents in Chile.

African Pentecostalism

African Pentecostalism owes its origins to the work of John Graham Lake (1870-1935), who began his ministry as a Methodist preacher but who later prospered in business as an insurance executive. In 1898 his wife was miraculously healed of tuberculosis under the ministry of Alexander Dowie, founder of the religious community called Zion City near Chicago. In 1907, Lake was baptized in the Holy Spirit and spoke in tongues.

Zion City also produced almost 500 preachers who entered the ranks of the Pentecostal movement. After his Pentecostal experience, Lake abandoned the insurance business to answer a long-standing call to minister in South Africa. In April 1908, he led a large missionary party to Johannesburg where he began to spread the Pentecostal message throughout the nation.

Lake succeeded in founding two large and influential Pentecostal churches in South Africa. The white branch took the name Apostolic Faith Mission in 1910, borrowing from the name of the famous mission on Azusa Street. David du Plessis, known to the world as "Mr Pentecost," came from this church.

The black branch eventually developed into the Zion Christian Church, which had six million members by 1993. Soon after Lake returned to the United States, the movement reached the Slavic world through the ministry of a Russian-born Baptist pastor Ivan Voronacv, who received the Pentecostal experience in New York City in 1919.

Through prophecies, he was led to take his family with him to Odessa, Ukraine in 1922. There he established the first Pentecostal church in the Soviet Union. Voronacv was arrested, imprisoned and martyred in a communist prison in 1943. The churches he founded survived extreme persecution and have become today a major religious force in Russia and the former Soviet Union.

Japan and Korea

Pentecostalism reached Korea through the ministry of Mary Rumsey, an American missionary who had been baptized in the Holy Spirit at Azusa Street in 1907. At that time, Rumsey believed that she was called to Japan and Korea.

It was not until 1928, however, that she landed in Korea. Before World War II, she had planted eight Pentecostal churches there before being forced out of the country by the Japanese. In 1952, those eight churches were turned over to the AG, whose missionaries immediately opened a bible school in Seoul.

One of the first students to enrol was a young convert by the name of Paul Yonggi Cho. After he graduated from bible college, Cho pioneered a Korean church that became the Yoido Full Gospel Church. By the time it had over 700,000 members it was heralded the largest single Christian congregation in the world.

As for the Neo-Pentecostals, Charismatics & Third Wavers - the first wave of the Pentecostal pioneer missionaries produced what has become known as the Classical Pentecostal Movement, with more than 14,000 Pentecostal denominations throughout the world.

This phase was followed by organized Pentecostal denominational mission efforts that produced fast growing missions and indigenous churches. The final phase was the penetration of Pentecostalism into the mainline Protestant and Catholic churches as *"charismatic renewal"* movements with the aim of renewing the historic churches.

New Waves

It is worth noting that these newer *"waves"* also originated primarily in the United States. They included the Protestant Neo-Pentecostal movement, which began in 1960 in Van Nuys, California, under the ministry of Dennis Bennett, Rector of St Marks Episcopal *(Anglican)* Church. Within a decade, this movement had spread to all the 150 major Protestant families of the world, reaching a total of 55 million people by 1990.

The Catholic Charismatic Renewal movement had its beginnings in Pittsburgh in 1967 among students and faculty at DuQuesne University. After spreading rapidly among students at Notre Dame and the University of Michigan, the movement spread worldwide.

In the subsequent years since its inception, the Catholic movement not only has gained the approval of the church but also has touched over 90 million Catholics in 120 countries. The newest category that was added to these was called the *"Third Wave"* of the Holy Spirit.

It originated at Fuller Theological Seminary in 1981 under the classroom ministry of John Wimber, founder of the Association of Vineyard Churches. This "wave" comprised mainline evangelicals who experienced sign and wonders but who disdained labels such as Pentecostal or Charismatic. The Vineyard was the most visible movement of this category. By 1990, the Third Wavers were credited with some 33 million members worldwide.

Evangelists & Healers

Throughout the previous century, Pentecostals produced many evangelists who were known for their mass healing crusades.

These included Maria Woodworth-Etter, Aimee Semple McPherson *(Founder of the International Church of the Foursquare Gospel in 1927)*, Oral Roberts, Kathryn Kuhlman, Reinhard Bonnke, Benny Hinn and Peter Youngren. Beginning in the 1950's with Oral Roberts, the "televangelist" genre appeared bringing healing, tongues, prophecies and other spiritual gifts into living rooms across the nation.

Some of the most successful ones included Pat Robertson's Christian Broadcasting Network and Paul Crouch's Trinity Broadcasting Network. Notable evangelists Jimmy Swaggart and Jim Bakker fell in the televangelist scandals of the 1980's.

Most religious and secular press carried news of the renewal. This was paralleled by the publication of millions of books and tapes sold in conferences and crusades internationally. New periodicals spawned by the movement included Dan Malachuk's *Logos* magazine and Stephen Strang's *Charisma and Ministries Today* magazines.

In the late 1970's a newer movement of *"faith"* teachers drew national attention. These included Kenneth Hagin Sr., Kenneth Copeland and Fred Price. In this 1990's millions of people tuned in to the teachings of Copeland and Price, while others enrol in Hagin's Rhema bible college in Broken Arrow, Oklahoma, and a host of other Spirit-filled bible schools.

Massive Crusades

Overseas, the crusades of the German Pentecostal evangelist Reinhard Bonnke regularly drew crowds of up to 500,000 in cities throughout Africa; *(then later on up to one million in one crusade; truly phenomenal!)* the same is true of Rev. Peter Youngren's crusades in India.

Major educational institutions arose during the 20th century as well. Healing evangelist Oral Roberts founded a university under his name in Tulsa, Oklahoma, in 1965, and Pat Robertson founded Regent University in Virginia Beach, Virginia, in 1978. In addition, liberal arts colleges and bible colleges were planted worldwide.

In a sense, the charismatic movement in the United States reached a peak in 1977 when 50,000 people from all denominations gathered in Arrowhead Stadium in Kansas City, Missouri, for the General Charismatic Conference led by Kevin Ranaghan. Planners for this conference were confronted by the major controversy of the era, which involved the *"shepherding"* teachings of four charismatic leaders from Fort Lauderdale, Florida: Derek Prince, Bob Mumford, Charles Simpson and Don Basham. This movement fell apart after the four separated in 1986.

Exotic Manifestations

In the 1990's, Pentecostals and Charismatics were re-invigorated by new waves of revival that featured such Pentecostal spiritual manifestations such as *"holy laughter," "falling under the Spirit,"* and other "exotic" manifestations.

Leading in this new wave was the South African Pentecostal evangelist Rodney Howard Browne. Beginning in 1993, manifestations appeared at the Toronto Airport Vineyard church led by Pastor John Arnott. Although Arnott's church was disfellowshiped by John Wimber and the Vineyard movement, the force of the revival has continued throughout the decade.

Another wave came in 1995 when a notable revival began at Brownsville Assembly of God in Pensacola, Florida. Led by Pastor John Kilpatrick and Evangelist Steve Hill, the Brownsville meetings have attracted more than two million visitors, and recorded almost 200,000 conversions.

Those resulting *"times of refreshing"* revealed at the end of the Pentecostal century that the movement was far from over and poised itself when entering the new millennium with undiminished power. Only time can reveal the true impact on the world that the Pentecostal movement had throughout the 20th century.

Finally - from the likes of Rev. Charles F. Parham, William J. Seymour, John Wesley, Thomas B. Barratt, John G. Lake, Alexander Dowie, Maria Woodworth-Etter, Aimee Semple McPherson, Oral Roberts, Kathryn Kuhlman, Reinhard Bonnke, Benny Hinn and Peter Youngren, Kenneth Hagin Sr., Kenneth Copeland and Fred Price, John Wimber, Pat Robertson, John Kilpatrick, Steve Hill to the infamous Rodney Howard Browne (the list is endless); everyone of these above mentioned gifts to the body of Christ had a responsibility to "catch" the baton held out to them.

Had they dropped their baton, then life, as we know it today, just wouldn't be the same! These men and women of God, epitomize what it is to *RUN WITH THE FAITH OF THE SON OF GOD*.

Signs of the Times

Take your everyday, ordinary life... and place it before God as an offering... **Don't become so well-adjusted to your culture that you fit into it without even thinking.**

(Romans 12:1 MSG)

The question that the last hundred years leaves us is this: **"What next?"** The only answer that can be given is that we must surrender to the move of the Holy Spirit and the authority of God's word! Only this marriage of God's Spirit and God's word will move us forwards in this generation.

Let me insert something here that came out during a conversation between Dr. Robb Thompson and Oral Roberts, which I happen to agree with very much indeed. In Oral's living room one day they began discussing how the Lord produced such great believers in the past. To which Brother Oral made the following comments:

> "IN THE LAST CENTURY – WE NEVER HEARD ABOUT THE WORD COMMITMENT. THE WORD WE CONSISTENTLY USED WAS SURRENDER."

I also would like to suggest that SURRENDER is a key word for any of us wanting to move on with the Holy Spirit today. We must learn once again what it means to be fully surrendered to the Lord.

In Psalms 37:7 it says "Surrender yourself to the LORD, and wait patiently for him. Do not be preoccupied..." (GW) However the Authorized Version uses the word "rest" in place of "surrender" here - which basically means to "stop yourself, to hold your peace and to quieten yourself!" (see Strong's #H1826)

To continue and to answer the question: "what next?" I will simply suggest that this has already begun taking place by what is known as **"The Apostolic and Prophetic Movement."**

Apostolic Ministries Formed

To qualify this point of view, let me add something that Roberts Liardon and I spoke about recently; he said, "The most successful students and ministers now come from schools that are birthed by Apostolic Ministries.

In the times of the reformation, seminaries were the place where great ministers were formed, but over time many of them have become places where God's word and the present day workings of the Holy Spirit are discredited. It seems that God has moved the place where He trains and launches His ministries and this increasingly is within the apostolic streams."

Church Historians

In addition to this, it's true to say that Church historians do recognize that the restoration of truth has been and is being restored to the church. You might say this began as far back as 1517.

We can recognize these individual movements according to a particular century and decade. But to summarize, **it is important to identify that the Church age could not be brought to a place of full maturity until the fivefold ministry gifts were restored,** that every one as a church member could be prepared to be part of a ministry team (i.e. a vehicle to reach society as seen in Ephesians 4:11–16).

These major truths have been restored:

- **Salvation by grace through faith** *(Ephesians 2:8-9)* was the beginning *(1500)*, which we now call *"The Protestant Movement."*

- In the 1600's *"The Evangelistic Movement"* began with water baptism and the separation of Church and State.

- In the 1700's *"The Holiness Movement"* came into being with sanctification, the Church being set apart from the world.

- In the 1800's *"The Faith Healing Movement"* with divine healing for the physical body and the recognition that healing was provided for in the atonement.

- In the 1900's *"The Pentecostal Movement"* exploded on the scene at a small bible school in Topeka, Kansas with former Methodist pastor Charles Fox Parham, with the Holy Spirit baptism, the evidence of speaking in tongues, and the gifts of the Spirit, the forerunners being Evan Roberts of the Welsh Revival *(1904)* and also William J. Seymour *(from 1906 onwards)* of the famous Azusa Street Revival USA.

- Then in the 1950's the *"Latter Rain Movement"* began with the prophetic presbytery, singing praises and melodious worship.

- Now from this time forth, *The Five Fold Apostolic Ministries* have been placed back in the Church, with recognition. *The Evangelist Ministry* and mass evangelism was reactivated.

- Then in 1960, *The Pastoral Gift* was restored to being the sovereign head of the local church, with renewal of all restored truth to all movement churches; this was known as *"The Charismatic Movement."*

- Then in 1970, *"The Faith Movement"* began with faith confessions, prosperity and victorious attitudes for life; with *The Teaching Ministry* re-established as a major *"five fold ministry."*

- In the 1980's we saw *"The Prophetic Movement"* begin with the prophet ministry restored and the company of the prophets brought forth. We also saw through this prophetic movement, a release of certain characteristics and revelations, such as the activation of warfare praise and prophetic intercession and much teaching on the Joshua generation, which challenged us to cross over into the Promised Land.

- Then in the 1990's *"The Apostolic Movement"* began with the **Apostle's ministry** being restored to bring divine order, structure and finality the restoration of the five fold ministries. Along with this gift, there have been fresh appearances of the miraculous, signs and wonders, unity amongst leaders and a great harvest of souls.

These are not competitive, controlling authorities, **but servant-hood** governments **that have come to serve the people of God and help them fulfil their course and purpose.** They will teach spiritual principles and not just mechanics of the word. They will understand that there are different mechanics for different things in different parts of the world.

However, the spiritual principles remain the same. These churches will train the people to use their unction and to follow the leading of the Holy Spirit to reap a bountiful harvest of souls, wherever they go in the earth.

Six Principles

The following five principles were inspired by Roberts Liardon's early teachings; the sixth principle is an addition!

- **Divine training takes place:** in a spiritual hub, you will find schools of training with divine purpose and commitment – a place where revelation will abound. Some of these schools will serve and minister to a particular territory; some will serve the nations.

- **Ministries are based in hubs:** it is a hub where travelling ministries base themselves. A ministry that succeeds and is effective in the earth must have a place of divine feeding, divine love, expectance and prayer.

- **Ministries and divine projects are launched:** it is a place where those who have prepared their hearts and lives are launched into spiritual position. There is an abundance of the word and the Spirit. Those who are truly called abound and prosper in the strength of their calling because of the environment of a spiritual hub.

  In this place, it is important to remember that because it is easy to feel called in a spiritual hub environment, we must search ourselves to make sure we have received the divine impartation to stand against the rough territories and to fulfil the commission or the path to which one is called.

- **Restoration for laity and ministries takes place:** for those who go out into the earth and build the works of God, it is good to have a place of refreshing where they can receive strength and help. It is wise to receive help when you need it, and to be renewed in your vision. If you are weary in well doing on the field, you must return to a place where you can be filled spiritually and encouraged.

- **It affects the culture of a city or a region:** the maturity, revelation and anointing of the churches in this Millennium will change the cities where they are based. Morality, crime and the economy will be positively affected. Cities where the Spirit of God rules strongly will grow and prosper. There are many testimonies given where churches have had major breakthroughs because of their *strong prayer and righteous mentality.* In some cases, bars have shut down, prostitution and crime to almost nil rate.

- **The pulling down of strongholds:** this has taken place because of the dealings with the principalities and powers over their territories. Dr. C. Peter Wagner says in his book *"Territorial Spirits"* that, *"evil spirits are assigned to geographical areas."* Let me make it plain, *these have to be pulled* down before we will see change and revival. Remember; time is a rewarder of faithfulness.

❖

CHAPTER 2

The Transition
into the 21st Century

Throughout church history there have been certain pioneers who have helped mark their generation for the Lord; leaving a legacy for others to follow. Commendable - but not many of those same pioneers were able to "transition" from one move of God to the next. The transition can be crucial and just as important as the pioneering efforts to begin with.

*I'm going to send you food from heaven like rain. Each day the people should go out and gather **only what they need for that day.** In this way I will test them to see whether or not they will follow my instructions...*

(Exodus 16:4-5 GW)

It is not my intention here to try and cover church history in this one short chapter, but I do however encourage you to go look for yourself and see what notable figures you can find of recent and not-so-recent within church history, who **"moved-on" when the Spirit of God began to blow a new wind of divine direction,** and made the transition into the new move of God. You will find those who made the transition and those who got lost because somehow the past had become their logos!

Cucumber Mentality

It is wonderful to be used of God, in any generation, but we must not get stuck. So that when God wants to do a new thing, we are not stubbornly attached to what He did in the past. Not many have been able to move on throughout church history, and notoriously prefer to stay with the familiar.

Consider the Israelites who were thinking of something as small-minded as **"onions and garlic"** when they were in the wilderness! Especially after experiencing all the adventure and enormity of God's deliverance, with the years of torment and suffering still fresh in their minds. Nonetheless they soon began to pine for the familiar.

Listen to their murmuring and contempt:

> *If only we had meat to eat! Remember all the free fish we ate in Egypt and the cucumbers, watermelons, leeks, onions, and garlic we had? But now we've lost our appetite! Everywhere we look there's nothing but manna!*
> *(Numbers 11:4-6 GW)*

Sadly this is a common human weakness; that we begin to crave the very thing that we were set free of! We become so familiar with the bondage that had us captive for so long, that we actually prefer it; a re-occurrence for us all especially if we stay in the wilderness.

It is true to say that not many people are able to experience God in their generation, *(pioneer, be in the forefront)* and then move on with Him and keep the impact on the next generation alive! Instead they get stuck in the last move... and don't know how to stay with what God is doing today.

We can call this the now move or wave of God *(which is relevant to any current generation...)* Most folks can only relate to their own experiences - so when something new happens - they can't flow with it. They miss it... lots of folks - even well intentioned folks miss God. *(It's easy to be "sincere" but "sincerely-wrong" at the same time!)*

Pioneers that made it!

By way of a short example I want to make mention of a few names that we are all so familiar with, those of recent church history; **pioneers such as Lester Sumrall, Morris Cerullo and Oral Roberts...** of course the list could go on.

Dr. Sumrall for instance **had the likes of Howard Carter and Smith Wigglesworth as his mentors and received some of their "anointing" for his generation.** He was ordained way back in 1932 and was considered the father of Christian Television because he helped secure the first license for 24-hour Christian television, amongst many other achievements.

But with all of his accolades Lester was one of those men *(of his calibre)* who did not get stuck in yesteryear... he moved on... and was one of the few who was able to do so. Right up until the end, he kept current with his finger on the pulse of what God was doing and saying in the now *(remember Hebrews 11:1 calls it "now-faith!")*

No Retirement for the Genuine

There is no retirement for genuine men and woman of God! They walk with God like Enoch did and then they are not..! They are too "black n white" to enjoy the "grey!" *(see Genesis 5:24)*

Lester Sumrall kept hearing God, keeping relevant to the day that he was in rather than aligning himself with the experiences of the past *(regardless of how successful they might have been)* he kept himself aligned to God. In fact the more successful a move may have been, can prevent folks from moving on to the next wave... somehow they imagine that God could only be successful in their generation - no matter how long ago that was - and don't ever move on because of that premise.

To qualify this, let me say that there is always a balance to everything. We are not talking about being politically correct or relevant in that context but in regards to what God is doing and saying today.

Dr. Sumrall was a good example for us to follow; not to get stuck in yesterday... but **stay hooked up with what God is saying and doing today.** If that means moving on from what we have known all our lives... moving away from the familiar - then yes... we must move on and not miss God. We must not get stuck in a generational or denominational rut!

If we refuse to move on with God, then what might have been successful in the past has now become a deception especially if it prevents us from hearing and moving on with God today.

Reading books and studying history can be of great value and is great in its place. BUT... if we are so caught up in the past, that we fail to hear God for today, then we have been caught in deception. **It takes a very brave man or woman - to move on with God. Especially if they helped pioneer the old!**

Yesterday and Today

Of course when we talk about what God is saying today this does not in any way change **His "Logos-word"** *(written)*... this always remains the same *"yesterday, today and forever."* However His **"Rhema-word"** - that which **He "speaks"** today - is fresh and is NOW manna. It never contradicts His written word. But it is for today. Otherwise we would all still be wearing sackcloth and ashes!!!

Let's make sure that we move with the tide, God's tide. Not with the popular opinion or political correctness of our day; but with God. **What is He saying right now? What is on His heart for our world right now?** If we know more about previous centuries and what God said to them, than we do today, then we have missed God for today.

Let's not make that same mistake that so many others have made and **move on** with God into the 21st century.

Nothing is holding us back. **We must make the "transition" into the apostolic,** which is only possible when we hear God's voice.

> *I am the good shepherd, and know my sheep, and am known of mine... they shall hear my voice...*
>
> (John 10:14-16 KJV)

❖

CHAPTER 3

A Network of Relationships

The Holy Spirit directs us to focus on building "spiritual relationships" so that a strong NETwork can be produced, relationships willing to work together for the purposes of the kingdom of God.

So then, as Christians, do you have any encouragement? Do you have any comfort from love? Do you have any spiritual relationships? **Do you have any sympathy and compassion?** *Then fill me with joy by having the same attitude and the same love, living in harmony, and keeping one purpose in mind.*

(Philippians 2:1-2 GW)

Such a network of relationships is *apostolic* in nature and is what the Holy Spirit continues to develop for this end time move of God. These relationships look for apostolic support and encouragement from other apostolic men and women of God in order to move forwards boldly and powerfully in the Holy Spirit; released to fulfil their destinies for the glory of God.

Networking People

A network literally means: a linking of people with a common interest or area of concern. Therefore as time develops, we will see a new emphasis on the development of such networks, working together across the board denominationally and via association. Networking does not imply that all groups should come under one "Pope" type figure, a specific apostolic movement, or "his holiness arch-bishop."

> Again, ***the kingdom of heaven is like unto a NET***, that was cast into the sea, and gathered of every kind: which, when it was full, they drew to shore, and sat down, and gathered the good into vessels, but cast the bad away.
> (Matthew 13:47-48 KJV)

Instead, kingdom networking simply involves associations and groups working together, just like large "fishing nets." This can be explained like so: each member of a network represents a single **KNOT** that helps tie the overall net together.

In addition, those with the grace, vision and wisdom enough, that is needed to network together with other networks - will eventually make up the greater fishing net that God will use to draw in the vast end time harvest of souls. A net that will both be large enough and strong enough to catch and to hold such multitudes!

Dr. Bill Hamon says of such networks, "This gives the Holy Spirit the opportunity to bring a greater unity and corporate vision within the body of Christ." This will enable all available resources to be harnessed to work together towards assisting the body of Christ to initiate and sustain an effective thrust towards souls. "The common meeting ground is to have the corporate vision of reaping the great end time harvest and proclaiming Jesus Christ as Lord over all the earth" (Hamon 14).

Nets to Equip

In the Amplified version of the above scripture (Matthew 13:47-48), it aptly uses the word DRAGNET: **"Again, the kingdom of heaven is like a <u>dragnet</u> which was cast into the sea and gathered in fish of every sort."** The Message Bible calls it a "fishnet" and the Authorized simply uses the word "net" as above.

The Greek word used for "net" does refer to fishing nets but also to PACKSADDLES, which in the East were simply bags made of *netted-rope*. However perhaps even more interesting is the Greek root meaning for the word "net" used in the Authorized, which means TO EQUIP! *(See Strong's #G4522 - also Matthew 4:19; 9:35; 13:49; John 21:1-ff; James 3:13; 4:1-8; 1 Peter 5:5-10).*

Therefore a strong and effective network largely depends upon the people involved *(especially pastors and leaders)* to be totally committed - in every aspect of their lives - to the Lord Jesus Christ. Cheerfully willing to pool their talents and abilities for the "over-all" without begrudging the personal cost.

Such relationships of association through networking are not meant to threaten or contradict denominational loyalties or even cause division; instead they are meant to assist, help bring strength, secure unity and a much greater clarity; especially in enhancing better skills in sharing the word of God.

One specific aim of a network is to help establish ministry centres of excellence and influence. Such can be called: *"Spiritually Governmental Hubs,"* that enhance God's kingdom and provide a significant "platform" *(for all the ministry gifts)* to speak into cities and nations with maximum effectiveness.

Such spiritual hubs help to develop ministries; enhancing and bringing them into positions of leadership that will influence every area of society. Utilizing skills individually and corporately to impact local regions as spheres of influence, for the *kingdom of God* and the glory of Jesus Christ.

Knots of Divine Appointments

Lastly let's take a look at the significance of knots, we could say that divine appointments are like "knots" in a net. They are **strong-connections** that can take the strain of apostolic relationships! In other words each relationship can be seen as a knot in the overall net. And any net is only as strong as its individual "knots" and "connections!"

Any fisherman will affirm that it's the knots that bring stability to the net and empower the net. Equally true for the kingdom of God, all of its knots *(divine connections and relationships)* strengthen its net. When such relationships *(knots)* are strong and in place they always breed more of the following: security, prosperity, encouraged abilities, healing, unity, trust and harmony.

> *Behold, how good and how pleasant it is for brethren to* **dwell together in unity!** *It is like the precious ointment upon the head, that ran down upon the beard, even Aaron's beard... for there the LORD commanded the blessing...*
> *(Psalm 133:1-3 KJV)*

FACT: fishermen spend a great portion of their time mending and cleaning their nets; perhaps more time than actually fishing! Likewise we too must spend larger portions of our time securing sound relationships that help develop the net - the kingdom! Only then will we be more effective.

FACT: fishing nets can catch vast amounts of fish, with a high percentage of what's caught being thrown directly back into the sea, *(wrong type or size!)* It's a stark reality that many "undesirables" will be caught in the kingdom's net, that will also be thrown back! **Even God is looking for a certain type of fish - that can be *gutted* correctly!**

Cleaned and Gutted

In other words, those ready to "give" themselves to the kingdom are kept and all else are thrown back. Those who are kept in the net (kingdom) are then "CLEANED" and "GUTTED!"

The emphasis in all of this is the "kingdom of God," as Matthew 13:47 clearly stated; **the kingdom of heaven is like a net..."** which was a direct teaching about the kingdom and not just a meagre net! In fact, including this particular parable about the NET, Jesus told **seven short parables** in total, about the kingdom of God.

- The Hidden Treasure - Matthew 13:44

- The Pearl of Great Price - Matthew 13:45-46

- The Yeast - Matthew 13:33-35, Luke 13:18-19

- The Mustard Seed - Matthew 13:31-32, Mark 4:30-34, Luke 13:18-19

- The Household Treasures - Matthew 13:52

- The Sprouting Seed - Mark 4:26-29

- **The Dragnet - Matthew 13:47-50**

So based on our knowledge of nets it's been easy to ascertain the basic characteristics of the kingdom; the restoration of the net equals the healing of relationships. Knots equal the need to submit one to another in effective cooperation and finally anyone who remains in the net *(kingdom)* will be cleansed and gutted!

Conclusion:

The kingdom of God is only as strong as its relationships *(knots!)* Making DIVINE NETWORKING a *major* part of kingdom activity. Therefore we must always be ready to work together, safe guarding strong and effective *connections* - with purity of heart - and a willingness to be steered by the larger plan and kingdom business of the Holy Spirit.

❖

CHAPTER 4

The Kingdom Reign of God

We have been looking at "knots" and how the New Testament referred to the kingdom of God as being like a "net." We looked briefly at the vital role of "knots" in a net and how they bring stability and strength. We talked about how each knot represented "divine relationships" or "contacts" within God's kingdom by using this powerful statement, "divine connections produce strong relationships that in turn develop and enhance God's kingdom."

Thy Kingdom come, Thy will be done, on earth as it is in heaven.

(Matthew 6:10 KJV)

So in keeping with this emphasis on the kingdom, let's move on to talk more about what the kingdom really is all about. To begin with, when the bible refers to the "kingdom of God," it is actually referring to the "reign" (authority) of God more than the "realm" over which He rules or over which His authority resides.

In other words, it is more about His authority than anything else! However in our modern day vernacular this has gotten a little lost, either in translation or in cultural references and we tend to assume that "kingdom" refers to a "place" or "territory" more than to "authority."

Clearly this makes it vital for us to correct our focus a little so that the true context is not lost and where we can properly adhere to the true meaning of kingdom as seen in scripture. That kingdom is essentially more to do with reigning, ruling and exercising authority than it is about the realm where that authority functions.

Predominant Meaning

I would say this is a far more dynamic concept. Much less passive! And it is within the New Testament that the predominant meaning of "kingdom" was God's reign or rule; with any other meaning seldom used.

For instance if we were to say, "the gospel of the kingdom of God," this would best be understood as *THE GOOD NEWS OF THE REIGN OF GOD.*" The gospel is the good news and the kingdom is His reign. Hence the good news of His reign! We must consider this and make it personal; His kingdom is His rule, His authority and His government, therefore when we receive the kingdom of God, we receive, accept His government and rule over our lives and hearts.

To solidify this concept, we can remember what Jesus said, that we must *"receive the kingdom of God like little children" (Mark 10:15)*. In other words, **we must receive the government of God over our lives in childlike trust,** because He has our best interests at heart. **Besides when He "governs" our lives, nothing else can!**

Consider this a little further. Every time we have prayed the "Lord's Prayer," we have actually petitioned God to reign over us, ("...thy kingdom come..." Matthew 6:10 KJV) The correct context being that "His will" must be obeyed on earth (by men) just as it is obeyed in heaven! Because when He is obeyed by men, and His will is done in this present life, then the kingdom of God has already come!

Obedience Enhances His Reign

It is already here! It is upon us! And obedience is always the key to truly dwelling in the kingdom of God. If we truly live in the kingdom of God NOW, by allowing Him to govern over us, this in turn must mean that we see the things of His kingdom coming to pass, not occasionally but regularly and routinely. We know that what is normal to the kingdom of God is not normal to this world (healings and miracles) but must be common-place to us!

When the bible was written, the hearers of the gospel possessed this early understanding of *"kingdom,"* and had a better grasp of its meaning than we do today. When they heard that the kingdom of God was at hand, they understood that it meant God's authority was being restored to the earth and that to enter the kingdom of heaven meant entering

God's reign and experiencing the benefits of this in our immediate lives.

Or perhaps today we would say in "real-time" which simply means "right-now!" Religion always keeps God "out-there" somewhere, but He and the rule of His kingdom is "right-here" and "right-now!"

Many preachers have told us that entering the "kingdom of heaven" means going to heaven when we die. While this is true, it leaves us with very little understanding of the purposes of God and His intentions for His Church. **Failure to preach and understand the "kingdom" of God is the reason that few Christians live the life of "OVER COMERS" today.**

Kingdom of God becomes a Present Reality

It is when the kingdom of God becomes a "present reality" and not just a "future hope," that mankind is able to enjoy the blessings of God's rule and reign in their individual lives. Where they enter the more abundant and victorious life that is promised in scripture, yet sadly is only enjoyed by a minority of Christians today.

Those who enjoy true kingdom benefits today are not some elite group who live opulent lifestyles, but rather those who have genuine "...*righteousness and peace and joy in the Holy Spirit,*" as mentioned in Romans 14:17. This IS the kingdom of God!

This is not to say that there is no future realm when Christ returns, but it opens to us the marvellous possibility that He will return to a world where His reign is already well established. Not to the fractured and feeble Church we have become, that is divided and has lost its grasp on what the true biblical concept of the kingdom really is.

When the kingdom of God is proclaimed to the Church and by the Church we will have returned to the original biblical truth of the matter. Even more importantly, we will be obeying the instruction of our King Jesus, **to proclaim the supernatural gospel of the kingdom of God, hastening the day of His return** (*see books by Dr. Myles Munroe – "Kingdom Principles" and "Rediscovering the Kingdom" – www.destinyimage. com*).

The kingdom of God is the only thing that Jesus ever called the "gospel." Few people understand this fact. And the fact remains that if we fail to proclaim the "gospel of the kingdom," we are not actually obeying His instruction to preach the "Good News of God's Reign and Authority!"

The government of God is the best news that anyone can ever hear, because it is God's only solution to all of man's ills. When we accept this "King Jesus" as the ultimate "ruler" of *every* aspect of our lives, then and only then can we truly experience kingdom living as it should be.

Ambassadors of His Kingdom

As ambassadors of His kingdom our role on this earth is to administer His kingdom justice here, His rule, reign and righteousness. This is the role of every single believer, to reign spiritually and administer His spiritual justice in order to put into affect His kingdom right here and right now.

To administer in the dictionary means to manage the affairs of, formerly give out, and to apply. This explains our role quite well in contemporary terms, because we have to minister into our everyday circumstances simply by applying God's spiritual truth and spiritual laws.

We do this without denying or breaching natural laws, in order to do things from a kingdom perspective! BUT **the laws of God's kingdom obviously supersede all others and we can apply these truths into the spiritual realm and let it take effect there.** Remember that everything originates in the spiritual realm first anyway (Genesis 1:1-2) and has its eventual effect here on the earth.

Take for instance such scriptures as Matthew 6:10 for example, where it says, "...as it is in heaven" and in Matthew 18:18 especially in the Amplified version where it talks about binding and losing on earth, just as it already is in heaven. **We are enforcers who enforce the things of God** but in the spirit realm FIRST. Because **that's where the struggle is, it is a spiritual battle and not one of flesh and blood (Ephesians 6:12).**

There are places of course where preaching is illegal and believers are forced underground but traditionally this has not hindered the gospel, on the contrary that's often when it runs the fastest, spreads hardest and supersedes all obstacles. But this is another discussion altogether!

What we are talking about here is applying God's spiritual truth into the atmosphere, letting it supersede all else; yet without breaching natural or political laws, to

the best of our ability! Remember just being righteous in an unrighteous world is spiritual warfare in itself. We don't have to open our mouths to create conflict, just being here – spiritually speaking - is conflict in itself! Remember we are light and light always disperses darkness.

Even our worship is warfare, because it creates an atmosphere that is "contrary" to the atmosphere of this world. Therefore even before we open our mouths, we are not welcome! Anything we engage in is spiritual warfare! Our very presence on earth creates a contradiction and a conflict. Essentially we represent a real and present "resistance" to evil – particularly when yielded to the Holy Spirit.

More Than Numbers

Dr. Paul Y. Cho in his book, **"More Than Numbers"** writes: "Since the beginning of recorded human experience, men have always tried to fathom an ideal society. Plato, the well-known Greek philosopher, that dreamed of an ideal society based upon an ethical political framework and social philosophies, that were too idealistic ever to be executed to his desired perfection.

The Old Testament prophets spoke of a future age when men would live together without armaments of war. Isaiah spoke of spears being turned into pruning hooks, and nations not lifting up swords against each other. In fact, the peace of the world would be so dramatically different that he used the images of a wolf lying down with a lamb, leopards with kids, and calves with young lions to signify the radical change in world affairs, which would come in the future.

The message, which Jesus preached, was one of repentance because the beginning of a new era was at hand. *'Repent, for the kingdom of heaven is at hand' (Matthew 4:17 KJV).* His teachings, illustrations, and parables were all primarily dealing with the kingdom of God. In fact the prayer he taught the disciples to pray was, *'Thy kingdom come, thy will be done on earth as it is in heaven' (Matthew 6:10 KJV).*

To the very end, Jesus continually emphasised the kingdom to his disciples. Although it is obvious to all who study the gospels that Jesus' main emphasis was on the kingdom of God *(Matthew called it the kingdom of heaven because he wrote primarily for the Jews),* I find little agreement on what the kingdom of God is and what the message of the gospel of the kingdom should be.

Synonymous to the Church

Augustine perceived the kingdom of God to be synonymous with the church. The Reformed movement had a large part in redefining the meaning of the kingdom of God. Calvin basically agreed with Augustine. He differed on what aspect of the church represented the kingdom of God. His feelings were that the true church, which was within the obvious church, was the earthly manifestations of the kingdom of God.

The task of the church would be made possible by the use of a special power called the gospel of the kingdom of God. This gospel of the kingdom of God would so affect the lives of first men and then nations that there would be a mighty transformation of social, political, and economic reality.

The church was likened to leaven which would slowly so permeate the dough of the earth that at a point in history the earth would proclaim Jesus Christ as Lord and King. At this point the Lord Jesus Christ would return to earth to accept the kingdom prepared for him by his heavenly Father.

There has been another school of theology, which does not try to explain the kingdom of God in terms of the future but tries to understand the kingdom of God in its present social context. *Harvey Cox* is just one of many modern theologians who view the kingdom of God as a social order brought about by the church.

The problems of inequality, prejudice, as well as the rest of our social concerns are to be addressed and dealt with by a church, which is conscious of its mission. Biblical terms are redefined to make them more relevant of today's problems. Many of our liberal church leaders are motivated by what they see is the lack of concern within the more conservative evangelical church leaders."

Basic Flaw of Theology

Cho continues, "Although my view of the kingdom of God will be given, I believe that there is a basic flaw in just a theological view of the kingdom of God. Although I believe in reason, I don't believe in reason's infallibility. There is a greater foundation than reason in establishing what the kingdom of God really is. That foundation is the simple and yet profound word of God. Let us look at some basic biblical principles, which will help us understand what the kingdom of God is.

The kingdom of God is not only for the future, but also for the present. *'For the kingdom of God is not meat and drink; but righteousness, and peace, and joy in the Holy Ghost'* *(Romans 14:17 KJV)*. Paul reveals to us that the kingdom of God transcends the natural existence of man and causes him to experience in the here and now, the fruit of the Holy Spirit. That if you associate with the Holy Spirit you will become like the person you are associating with.

The natural result of association with the Holy Spirit will be a way of life, which is more concerned with the quality God bestows to life rather than the essential aspects to life, eating and drinking.

Changing Sides

Paul also reveals that the kingdom of God is something that we have entered into as a result of our being regenerated by the Holy Spirit. *'[God] hath delivered us from the power of darkness, and hath translated us into the kingdom of his dear Son'* *(Colossians 1:13 KJV)*. The word, *'translated,'* used in our English text, in the Greek is *metestasen,* which literally means to change sides.

As I study this verse, I see a picture of a football game. Each team is on the opposite end of the field. On one side is the team, which represents the kingdom of darkness. On the other side is the team, which represents the kingdom of God. During the game, one of the main players of the darkness team takes off his shirt and number, goes to the opposing bench and puts on the kingdom of God shirt. Then he goes on the field to play against the darkness boys. He simply switches sides. This is what happened to us. We were transformed from one kingdom to the other, the kingdom of our Lord.

The kingdom of God is also described in its future prospect for eternal blessedness:

> *Wherefore the rather, brethren, give diligence to make your calling and election sure: for if ye do these things, ye shall never fall: For so an entrance shall be ministered unto you abundantly in the everlasting kingdom of our Lord and Saviour Jesus Christ.*
>
> *(2 Peter 1:10-11 KJV)*

In Matthew Jesus spoke of the future when he said, *'Many will come from the east and west and sit at the table with Abraham, Isaac and Jacob in the kingdom of heaven'* (8:11). Yet in Matthew 13, our Lord tells parables which give further clarification to what he meant by the kingdom of heaven. He says that once the kingdom is purged, the righteous would shine like the sun.

Jesus is the representation of what it is like to be in the kingdom. *'The kingdom of God is not coming with signs to be observed; nor will they say, 'Lo, here it is!' or 'There!' for behold, the kingdom of God is in the midst of you'* (Luke 17:20-21 RSV).

This verse can be applied to the fact that the kingdom of God was there in their midst. The *'you'* here is the plural, which in English is hard to understand. Jesus was there in there midst. The Pharisees were not to look for a glorious manifestation in the future, but the kingdom was before them and they were too blind to observe that God was working without a lot of fanfare.

The Kingdom Paradox

The kingdom's paradox has to be viewed on the basis of a balanced understanding. Jesus told Pilate in John 18, *'My kingdom is not of this world.'* Yet he also said in Luke 13 that the kingdom of God would start out rather unobservable, like a mustard seed. Yet, this seed, almost unnoticed, would grow up and affect the entire world.

Rather than seeing opposing views in scripture as contradictory, I consider them as a balance. **Therefore, the kingdom of God is *future*, but it is *present*. It is not of this world, but it affects this world. It can be entered into at the present time, but there is a future fulfilment. You can't see it with the natural eye, but the kingdom of God is everywhere Christ is.**

As we analyse the kingdom further we realise that the word kingdom can be understood in different ways.

Both the word *baileia,* the Greek word translated kingdom; and the Hebrew word *malkuth* signify the rank and authority exercised by a king. Our present thinking deals with the people who are under the king's authority or the actual territory over which kingly authority is exercised. So the nature of the authority may be closer to the understanding of the biblical concept of kingdom than the actual subjects of the authority.

Psalm 145:13 expresses in poetic terms something of this idea, *'Thy kingdom is an everlasting kingdom, and thy dominion endureth throughout all generations.'* In classical

Hebrew poetry, the two verses of the poem are to express the same idea in differing ways. Therefore the poet's concept of the kingdom was that it was God's actual dominion.

Kingdom Legitimacy

Herod the Great was not a popular king of Israel. Although he rebuilt the temple to majestic grandeur and built a great many fine public buildings in Jerusalem, he had no real kingdom. There was no genuine basis for his authority apart from Roman might. He had gone to Rome and had been given the kingship over Israel without a legitimate basis for having this kind of authority.

He was not born to it. A recognised prophet did not anoint him. He was not a descendant of Judah. He had no legitimacy. Although he lived in a palace, wore a crown and was called King Herod, his kingdom was bought and not earned. In Great Britain there are estates that can be bought which will carry a title with them. So if you have enough money, you may buy a title. Yet, this is not the same as being given a title by the queen, or being born into a noble family. Money might buy you a title, but that title is not legitimate.

As we analyse this thinking further, it causes us to understand the prayer, which Jesus told us to pray: *'Thy kingdom come. Thy will be done in earth, as it is in heaven.'* More than asking God to take over the world in a cataclysmic event, there seems to be the desire in the heart of the Lord for the authority of God to be as obvious to the earth as it is obvious in heaven.

Conclusion:

Therefore I believe that the kingdom of God is the nature of His reign or His authority. It is genuine, it is indisputable, and it is eternal. The reign of God is present, but it will also be in the future. God has always been in charge! He is the Creator of the earth and for that matter the entire universe. He is all-powerful.

However, in this human arena called earth, God has allowed Himself to be limited. Satan was given a realm of authority; he is the god of this present age. He has authority over this world's systems. His seat of authority is in the immediate atmosphere surrounding the world.

God has provided an escape from the territory over which Satan has authority. He provided Jesus Christ, the last Adam" (Cho 77-81).

❖

CHAPTER 5

The Church Age Begins

Bob Walker in 1952 prophesied, that the Assemblies of God and other Pentecostals had planted the seeds of a mighty "Charismatic" revival. He stated that soon the revival would break out in all denominations. **It has come to pass.** We are now seeing the end-time outpouring of the Spirit.

Satan is raging. We are at war. But the prophet said, *"that when the enemy comes in like a flood the Spirit of God will raise up a standard against him."* One of the greatest dangers facing the Evangelicals, Pentecostals and Charismatics is a rejection of our biblical heritage and radical changes of our views on the end-times. The non-Kingdomists and Dominionists are examples of this. New and extreme winds of doctrine seem to blow around us with gale force. Nevertheless many stand firm and proclaim God's truth for these last days. Indeed, we are *"set for the defence of the gospel."*

Earnestly contend for the Faith

After Jesus' death and resurrection came the Day of Pentecost, the Holy Spirit was poured out and the church was born.

The church grew, thousands of Jews believed that Jesus of Nazareth was the Messiah, and that His death and resurrection was exactly what the prophets had foretold. Many went out as Jesus had commanded them *(Matthew 28:19)*, "Go into all the nations." The result was that even Gentiles were professing Jesus Christ as their Lord. Questions arose among Jewish believers about whether the Gentile believers were required to keep the Mosaic Law or not?

Tensions grew between Jewish and Gentile Christians led early to each side, having to define in great discussion their relationship regarding both the Law and circumcision. The Gentile believers should simply abstain from certain kinds of food, such as blood and from fornication *(Acts 15)*.

For the Jews both the Abrahamic and the Mosaic covenants had the same validity, and it was unthinkable to interpret history with its promises in an allegorical or spiritual manner.

Neither Jesus nor the apostles denied the historical testimony of the Old Testament but they gave its texts an added perspective. Paul described the Non-Jewish believers as branches, taken from a wild fruitless olive tree *(the heathen nations)*, and grafted into cultivated, fruitful olive tree with a nourishing sap filled root *(Israel)*.

> *If some of the branches have been broken off and you though a wild olive shoot have been grafted in among the others and now share in the nourishing sap from the olive root, do not boast over those branches. If you do, consider this: you do not support the root, but the root supports you.*
>
> *(Romans 11:17-18)*

Despite Paul's explicit warning to the Gentile churches not to boast against the *"Fathers"* and the *"root,"* i.e. the Jewish people, it was not long before the official church developed the theology that God had completely rejected *"old Israel"* and replaced it with the *"church."* All the promises in the Old Testament were taken to mean the "church" in the capacity of *"the new Israel."*

Greek Gnosticism secured a foothold in the church, by means of various rites, as did Babylonian mystery cults. Struggles for power by certain bishops also had an effect, as well as local superstitions. Then in the fourth century the Roman Caesar Constantine, declared that the struggle against Christianity was lost. So he proclaimed religious freedom throughout the Roman Empire and Christianity was declared the official religion.

The Religious World Opposes Revival

The Church became an institution for authoritarian politics, this in turn developed into the Roman Catholic and Greek Orthodox religions we know today. Religion, supremacy, legends, superstitions and human traditions gained power, but Christianity gradually disappeared. Mariology and veneration of saints came increasingly to the forefront within society. This seemingly brought a twofold development that led an assault against bible-based revival movements and against Jews.

After Christianity was accepted by the State, it became distorted. Doctrines on grace, faith, repentance and salvation were perverted. Repentance from the heart and the new birth were no longer emphasised. People believed that God's grace was obtained through the sacrament — infant baptism, communion, confirmation, confession, marriage, priesthood, ordination, and finally, extreme unction.

It was said you could only become a Christian by doing all these things! The most sacred was infant baptism. It was taught that an infant was born again through water baptism, as God's Spirit was imparted through the water. Then as the child grew and participated in the various sacraments within the church system, then the child was a Christian.

Biblical Revelation

Assurance of salvation was lost, the result, an enormous doctrine of works, which combined various occult elements. The forming of *"holy orders"* and *"holy places"* with *"holy objects," "saints."* All these were nothing more than man's contrived attempts to reach God and obtain His approval.

Many superstitions began to flourish together with the worship of saints, fetishes, fables, myths and unbiblical traditions. Biblical revelation was lost and withheld from ordinary people who were lost in a maze of condemnatory fabrications and superstitious beliefs. Holy lifestyles and reverence for God were lost and replaced by liturgy, pilgrimages, flagellation, monks and holy orders. Candles and crucifixes became holy objects. Icons became an occult medium through which it was said, life and grace were imparted from heaven. As the papacy developed so too did the worship of saints *(ancestor worship)*, and Mariology. Latin became a holy language and the liturgy was read with Latin prayers like occult incantation.

Religion had now taken over, New Testament Christianity had lost its power, extinguished by demonic imitation, the life had gone.

Replacement Theology

Unbiblical features became part of the norm as the church moved away from its Jewish and biblical roots. As Christianity was proclaimed the official religion of the Roman Empire, becoming legal requirement, replacement theology became increasingly prevalent.

A false charge has echoed from this time, with lasting accusation, the Jews are still being charged with the same violent attacks. This accusation is the most serious because it has theological root. ***Did the Jews murder Jesus?***

Augustine *(354 to 430AD)* systematically developed, *"Kingdom Now Theology."* He did this with reference to the theology of the kingdom of God, applying this to the Jewish thinking about themselves as God's kingdom. Augustine developed the thought that their dispersion *(the Jews)* was a sign to Christians who when they saw what had befallen the Jewish people who had rejected and murdered Jesus, their own Messiah. This then would be a warning concerning what would happen to anyone falling away from the church — the *"Mother"* of all believers.

He also argues that the church's interpretations of the Old Testament injunctions are shadows. He maintains that these shadows become realities in the new life Christ gives! Declaring that the Old Testament is a prophecy concerning Christ, and therefore Christians now possess all the promises contained therein. The application is that the *"church"* is in itself an institution, and the *"Heavenly State"* to be — set up on earth.

Fugitive Status and Vagabonds

Furthermore all Jews were condemned to fugitive status, vagabonds wondering the earth as punishment for putting to death Christ. This fever had now spread the excitement of a fight and being in good stead for it was a new phenomenon. The theologians and so-called church fathers who were to be examples, Christ like, were also involved and quick to embrace anti-Semitism.

Because of the anti-Semitic view many people shut the Jews out, unless of course they became Christians like everyone else. Some treated this as a new fad, meaning that everyone else was *"doing it,"* like the latest fashion. The question was and is: **Did the Jews murder Jesus? Was it justifiably, biblical?**

Let's find out.

First: the Roman authorities sentenced Him to death and the Roman soldiers carried out the execution. According to history both Romans and Jews were involved, so to be consistent all Romans and Italians and Jews ought to be persecuted.

Second: theologically speaking Jesus was to be the Lamb who would be sacrificed for the sins of all mankind. Sinners then killed Him! Jesus repeatedly told His disciples that He had to go to Jerusalem to suffer and die there. Much earlier John the Baptist had prophesied over Him saying, "Look the Lamb of God who takes away the sin of the world" *(John 1:29)*. When Peter tried to defend Jesus' life with a sword in Gethsemane, Jesus declared:

> *Do you think I cannot call on my Father, and he will at once put at my disposal more than twelve legions of angels? But how then would Scriptures be fulfilled that say it must happen in this way?*
> *(Matthew 26:53-54)*

Jesus also said:

> *The reason my Father loves me is that I lay down my life — only to take it up again. No one takes it from me, but I lay it down of my own accord. I have authority to lay it down and authority to pick it up again. This command I received from my father.*
> *(John 10:17-18)*

Third: is there any room for hatred towards the Jews? The bible says in 1 Corinthians 13:5 that Love... keeps no record of wrongs. Persecution, personal hatred, revenge has no place in a believer's heart. The Jews are not eternally damned; God loves them as He does the entire world. **The Jewish people will always be in God's plan.**

When you pass through the waters, I will be with you; and when you pass through the rivers, they will not sweep over you. When you walk through the fire, you will not be burned; the flames will not set you ablaze.

(Isaiah 43:2)

Since you are precious and honoured in my sight, and because I love you, I will give men in exchange for you, and people in exchange for your life. Do not be afraid, for I am with you; I will bring your children from the east and gather them from the west.

(Isaiah 43:4-5)

I ask then, did God reject his people? By no means! I am an Israelite myself, a descendant of Abraham, from the tribe of Benjamin. God did not reject his people, whom he fore knew. Don't you know what the Scripture says in the passage about Elijah — how he appealed against Israel?

(Romans 11:1-2)

I believe the question is answered,
No one took the life of Jesus!
"He gave it."

❖

CHAPTER 6

Replacement Theology

We know that Replacement Theology is prevalent in all Christian groups to some degree, but to one man's experience it became too much to bear — Martin Luther *(1483-1546)*. Luther protested about Replacement Theology by nailing a 95-page thesis to the church door at Castle Church, Wittenberg, on 31st October 1517.

The veil was lifted when he received a revelation on Romans 1:16-17, like a flashing light.

I am not ashamed of the gospel, because it is the power of God for the salvation of everyone who believes: first to the Jew, then to the Gentile.

For in the gospel, righteousness from God is revealed, a righteousness that is by faith from first to last.

He realised that righteousness; peace, justification and mercy were not earned through man's efforts or religious deeds. God imparts them through Christ's sacrifice on the cross. Everything he has done for us on the cross, He works in us when we received Christ Jesus. *"For we maintain that a man is justified by faith apart from observing the Law"* (Romans 3:28).

Up to this point in his life he was a Roman Catholic, a monk, with all its teachings on works, superstitions, human traditions and church politics. Doctrines on grace, faith, repentance and salvation were perverted. Repentance from the heart and New birth was no longer emphasised. People believed that God's grace was obtained through the sacraments — infant baptism, communion, confirmation, confession, and priesthood.

Luther a monk, then priest, and later Professor of Theology, was hoping to find peace with God through all his good works, but the opposite was true. He religiously fasted and prayed to Mary and the saints. He wore horsehair shirts, made regular confessions and pilgrimages, and bought indulgences hoping to find peace with God. But it was seemingly futile.

During this period Luther visited Rome, Christianity's religious capital. He staunchly prayed, fasted and gave alms. He even walked on his knees praying on Sancta Scala. He did everything in his power to please God, yet he remained empty inside.

When he gradually became aware that the whole religious system to which he belonged was absolute, he intended to reform it. He began to realise that the church had totally perverted the gospel. Legalistic works had replaced the gospel of grace; faith had been substituted by superstition and religious actions. Human legends, traditions and the Canon Law had replaced the bible. Instead of the outworking of the word and the Spirit through ministerial gifts, there were Popes, Cardinals, Bishops and Priests whose word took precedence over the bible.

Selling indulgences was particularly loathsome to Luther. The church taught that monks and priests could be paid to pray for the souls of the dead. The Pope at the time, proclaimed a special indulgence called *"Peter's penny"* which was used to build St. Peter's in Rome.

This money, recovered through this indulgence, was supposedly to save your relative years of suffering in purgatory.

The Reformation is Born

The reformation is born! The grip of Catholicism over Europe was giving way to this restoration of teaching. And Luther was excommunicated and out-lowed by the Catholic church.

Luther who God had used and was diligent in his cause also fell into *"Replacement Theology."* Like the Catholic theologians, Luther had interpreted all the promises of salvation in the Old Testament as fulfilled in Christ. The belief is salvation, which the Old Testament saints held, is what is known as ***"anticipated belief in Christ."*** In other words, the Christian Church is also anticipated in the Old Testament. This is true and in accordance with the witness of the New Testament but if one by reasons thinks that the role of the Jews in God's plan of salvation is concluded, then one is *"walking in darkness and does not know where one is going."*

Postulations of the anti-Jewish kind by Luther once fuelled the Catholic church in its persecution of the Jews, can be summed up as follows:

- God's judgmental wrath abides upon unbelievers and He alone can annul it. God Himself has appointed the Jews to judgement as punishment for what they did to his Son Jesus.

- Jews cannot repent of their own free will. There is no way in which they can be brought into the church; they are stiff-necked unbelievers and incurable despite all efforts to help them.

- Their continual blasphemy of Christ and God proves their religions to be still alive but hostile toward God.

- This appointed suffering abides likewise upon other enemies of Christ and God. The Israelites rejection of Christ is constantly being repeated within Christianity, and the Jews personify the belief, which is perpetually breaking out within the church (Maurer 56).

Bitter controversy was the result of three connected writings produced by Luther in 1542-1543.

He wrote, "A man who doesn't know the devil may well wonder why the Jews above all others, are so hostile towards

Christians. Moreover, they are so without cause, for we show them all goodness. They live here among us and have the use of our land, streets and lanes while our leaders are still sitting back, snoring open-mouthed, allowing them to lift from their purses and coffers, and to steal and rob them as they fancy. How? By allowing their own subjects and themselves to be fleeced and impoverished by the usury of the Jews, and so, with their own money, they make themselves beggars."

Luther in giving proposals to Evangelical leaders of the day said, *"They dishonour God and worship the devil when they, in their blasphemous fables, make Christ out to be a witch-doctor."* And all the atrocities which had been ascribed to the Jews such as poisoning water, child-stealing, blood-guiltiness were probably true. He suggested that the Jewish houses should be demolished and the occupants removed to temporary huts built by gypsies. There right to safe-conduct should be abolished prohibition of usury, slave labour for able-bodied Jews and Jewesses and the burning of all synagogues and Jewish schools.

Thankfully there was some sanity among those Evangelical leaders, one cannot help thinking where the Love of Christ was, where Luther was concerned!

The Jews account Luther as one of history's worst anti-Semites. They consider him as one who laid the foundation for the extermination of the Jews during the Second World War.

Through the preaching of the clergy, the church was not only compliant with, but in many cases supportive of, anti-

Jewish tendencies in the Third Reich. One of Hitler's leading men, Streichner defended the extermination of the Jews at the Nuremberg trials by quoting from Martin Luther's writings!

In conjunction with the celebration of Luther's 500th anniversary, the Lutheran World Council issued the following statement:

"We Lutherans can neither accept nor overlook the vehement verbal assaults made by the Reformer upon the Jews... Luther's sinful anti-Jewish statements and his fierce attack upon the Jewish people must be acknowledged with deep sorrow. All possibility of similar aggression, both now and in the future, must be removed from our churches."

❖

CHAPTER 7

Laying Foundation

Many years ago I was ordained a "bishop" and this is just one of the *titles* that I have gained over the years but I have certainly not chased titles, rather they have chased me! However through the process of my own personal journey I have discovered the importance of such titles, simply because God gave specific gifts to the church and we *must* be able to recognise, *who is who*.

> *Built on the foundation of the apostles and prophets, with Christ Jesus Himself as the chief cornerstone. In Him the whole building is joined together and rises to become a holy temple in the Lord. And in Him you too are being built together to become a dwelling in which God lives by his Spirit.*
>
> *(Ephesians 2:20-22)*

God is not the author of confusion; He knows exactly who he has anointed to serve the purposes, what *gifts* He bestowed on each and exactly how they should operate *(not excluding how others should address or recognise them!)*

Even though many *extremes* exist out there, this is still not reason enough to *totally* dismiss or be in denial about God's gifts for the local church. When we behave like this it is either out of fear or just plain unbelief! In fact many have chosen to *discourage* the use of such titles, based exclusively on their own perceptions and then taught such *perceptions (perceived truths)* to the rest of the body. But this is not based upon the word of God, as scripture itself is very clear concerning the correct use of titles.

Avoiding Error

This means that the very people who attempt to avoid error concerning titles, end up embracing it and then propagating it! All because it feels more *acceptable!* This type of *"replacement theology"* occurs when people literally *"replace"* truth for what allows them to stay within the confines of their own religious comfort zones!

Of course all of us cannot go further than what we have been taught or that which has been revealed to us personally by the Holy Spirit. For example, in the Faith Movement everybody is considered a "pastor!" But in the Evangelical Movement there is a greater emphasis on "eldership" and having a "set" minister.

So generally speaking, there is wide recognition for the pastoral gift, the evangelistic gift and the teacher, but when it comes to the apostle and prophet, they are commonly denied or ignored! People tend to forget that Jesus was indeed our apostle and high priest; with many more titles besides, but not least our *apostle!*

> *Therefore, holy brothers, who share in the heavenly calling, fix your thoughts on **Jesus, the apostle and high priest** whom we confess.*
>
> *(Hebrews 3:1)*

I can share from personal experience, that when I travel throughout Europe, it's easier to use the word *apostle* than *bishop!* Yet when I travel throughout the African churches, there is a much greater emphasis on the "bishops," who are held in great esteem, while all others are perceived as being beneath such *hierarchy.*

Diocese Episcopate

I would suggest that this is a little backward! Yet I'm not saying we should now throw-the-baby-out-with-the-bath-water and get rid of all the bishops. Not at all! Though correct and balanced teaching *must* be brought back into the church, especially where leadership positions and titles are concerned. Now if the anointing flows *down* and not up, this means that church leaders must get this accurate or the rest of the body will be confused.

There is nothing in this system, which corresponds exactly to the modern diocese episcopate; bishops, when they are mentioned *(Philippians 1:1)* are from a board of local congregational officers and the position occupied by

Timothy and Titus is that of Paul's personal lieutenants in his missionary work. It seems most likely that he was then specially designated with the title of bishop; but even when the monarchical bishop appears in the letters of Ignatius, he is still the pastor of a single congregation.

The word **episkopos** occurs five times in the NT: once of Christ *(1 Peter 2:25)* and in four places of "bishops" or **"overseers" in local churches** *(Acts 20:28; Philippians 1:1; 1 Timothy 3:2, Titus 1:7)*. The verb **episkopeo** occurs in Hebrews 12:15 *("watching")* and *(in some NT MSS)* 1 Peter 5:2 *("exercising the oversight")*.

A bishop then has "oversight of," he is an "overseer." 1 Peter 5:2 says, "Feed the flock of God which is among you, taking the oversight thereof" *(KJV)*. The Greek word for "oversight" is **episkopeo,** Strong's #G1983 - to oversee, to beware, to look diligently, take the oversight. Extra words given: direction *(about the times)*, have charge of, take aim at *(spy)*, regard, consider, take heed, look at *(on)*, mark.

Take for instance when I was on a ministry trip to Africa, I was asked to be involved in a *presbytery*, during a particular ordination service. Some of those individuals to be ordained that day, I might add, were accomplished men in their own right, one in particular was acting chaplain to a very high-ranking government official within his own country and was held in high regard himself.

However during the process of this extremely ceremonial meeting, they proceeded to make such a fanfare of these prospective bishops, to the point that it was almost ridiculous! The last person they ordained that day was a woman evangelist, whom they ordained as an apostle and whom they gave very little prominence to at all. **They clearly misunderstood the *governing role* and *office* of an apostle, versus the general *overseeing role and office* of a bishop,** *(I had the unpleasant job of trying to straighten out their theology before I left).*

However we cannot allow *confusion* to reign unchallenged, in the body of Christ, especially concerning such important matters as these. This fuels my passion even more, to help *restore* some clarity back into the church, about the true position, nature and role of the apostle; in regards to the other five-fold-ministry gifts, as well as putting the record straight about "bishops" who were originally and basically commissioned as "overseers" for the local-church!

Apostolic and the Prophetic

Only by turning to scripture can we reveal the true *position-that-goes-with-the-title* and show up whether or not certain "replacement doctrine" has crept into the church. Again, once error is embraced, it readily circulates throughout the rest of the body like a virus that must be stopped and corrected!

It's important for us to realise that we are currently in the move of the apostolic and the prophetic - so let's define the gift of *apostle* in particular and whether such a gift truly exists today! **Please at this point - don't decide that titles do not matter, they do have their place, even today!**

Consider Paul in whose writings he often declared himself, "Paul an apostle." Why? Because Paul knew exactly who he was and what he was commissioned to do. This should be true of the rest of us, because there is clear foundation and structure to the body of Christ, which Jesus Himself put into place.

❖

CHAPTER 8

The Objective of an Apostle

By the grace God has given me, I laid a foundation as an expert builder, and someone else is building on it. But each one should be careful how he builds... *(1 Corinthians 3:10) Strong's #G753 architekton (ar-khee-tek'-tone); from 746 and 5045; a chief constructor, i.e. architect, KJV - **masterbuilder**.*

Let's look at the following 5 objectives:
The First Objective of an Apostle:

He is more than just an architect; He is like a "superintendent" of the building process. *Strong's #G5045 tekton (tek'-tone); from the base of 5098: an artificer (as producer of fabrics), i.e. (specifically) a **craftsman** in wood: KJV - carpenter.*

This apostolic function is the necessary basis for every local church, which forms part of the household of God.

77

"Consequently, you are no longer foreigners and aliens, but fellow citizens with God's people and members of God's household, **built on the foundations of the apostles and prophets,** with Christ Jesus Himself as the chief cornerstone" *(Ephesians 2:19-20).*

Secondly He Lays a Foundation of Life in Christ:

By the grace God has given me, I laid a foundation as an expert builder, and someone else is building on it. But each one should be careful how he builds. For no one can lay any foundation other than the one already laid, which is Jesus Christ.

(1 Corinthians 3:10)

This is done very importantly via the word of truth but also by fatherly relationship. In other words, it's not just achieved by endless impersonal teachings; "For though ye have one thousand instructors in Christ, yet have ye not many <u>fathers</u>: for in Christ Jesus I have begotten you through the gospel" *(1 Corinthians 4:15 KJV).*

Note: speakers only have *hearers,* **where fathers have** *children!* A father-in-the-faith is not a remote and austere figure that separates himself from the people but is *real* and *approachable,* just as a father with his son.

However even though an apostle takes on that fatherly role, another major emphasis must be established here, that an **apostle is a BUILD-ER** and not just a **BLESS-ER!** For example he is not easily given to emotions and shallow-short-term-solutions, *(which are often miss-represented as "blessing!")*

No! He is in it for the *long-term* and is willing to go the extra mile with people, in order to *build* something substantial into their lives. In other words, an apostle is never committed to the popular **"hit-n-run"** or **"quick-fix"** solutions, but sticks with the process until he sees real fruit appear in people's lives! **"My dear children, for whom I am again in the pains of childbirth *until* Christ is formed in you..."** *(Galatians 4:19)*

Third, He Lays a Foundation of Obedience towards Christ:

He stresses clearly from the beginning the Lordship of Jesus Christ for whom he is pledged to make disciples. He aims to bring about the "obedience of faith" and looks for that obedience to be complete.

> *Through him and for his name's sake, we received grace and apostleship to call people from among all the Gentiles to the obedience that comes from faith.*
>
> *(Romans 1:5)*

One definite fact is that it's hard to get away with *anything,* when an apostle is around! His aim is to help each individual in the church to build his house upon the only sure foundation of obedience - the commandments of Jesus.

> *Then Jesus came to them and said, "All authority in heaven and on earth has been given to me. Therefore go and make disciples of all nations, baptizing them in the name of the Father and of the Son and of the Holy Spirit, and teaching them to obey everything **I have commanded** you. And surely I am with you always, to the very end of the age."*
>
> *(Matthew 28:18-20)*

*Therefore everyone who hears these words of mine and puts them into practice is like a wise man who **built his house** on the rock...*

(Matthew 7:24)

Fourthly, He Lays a Foundation of Doctrine:

Before the church can go on to maturity, the foundational doctrine must have been clearly laid. **This is the responsibility of the APOSTLE not the bishop.** To build and to work, making sure that every member of the church is clear on repentance and faith, baptism in water and the Holy Spirit; on eternal judgment and the resurrection from the dead.

*Therefore let us leave the elementary teachings about Christ and go on to **maturity**, not laying again the foundation of repentance from acts that lead to death, and of faith in God, instructions about baptisms, the laying on of hands, the resurrection of the dead, and eternal judgment. And God permitting, we will do so.*

(Hebrews 6:1-3)

He will establish them on the same sure foundation of their death and resurrection with Christ.

*So then, just as you received Christ Jesus as Lord, continue to live in Him, rooted and **built up in Him**, strengthened in faith as you were taught, and overflowing with thankfulness.*

(Colossians 2:6-7)

He confirms in them the dynamic of what it means to be united with Christ *(Romans 6:1ff)*. He contends with every error and distortion that would detract from the fullness of Jesus and diminish the believer's fullest experience of Him.

> *See to it that no-one takes you captive through hollow and deceptive philosophy, which depends on human tradition and the basic principles of this world rather than on Christ. For in Christ all the fullness of the Deity lives in bodily form, and you have been given fullness in Christ, who is the Head over every power and authority.*
> *(Colossians 2:8-10)*

Legalism, asceticism, mysticism and pseudo-spirituality are all refuted and corrected. The word of God is for the apostle, the *only* existing basis for building.

Five, The "master-builder" is responsible for the whole construction and supervises the entire work:

He is especially concerned for the fitting-out of the building for its intended use. A house must be finished so that the occupants can take up residence.

An apostolic leader is equally concerned for the house of God. He sees that the parts of the building are fitted and equipped to serve their function. All this is so that the church may once more be a dwelling place fit for God and his Holy Spirit *(Ephesians 2:20).*

❖

CHAPTER 9

Types of Apostles

In this particular chapter we are going to clearly differentiate between the two *major* types of apostles *(as there are others, such as regional or international apostles and so forth)*. However to begin with the word apostle means: "to-send-forth;" someone with a commission to fulfil; representing the same authority that sent them.

> *Paul, an apostle - __sent__ not from men nor by man, but by Jesus Christ and God the Father, who raised him from the dead...*
>
> *(Galatians 1:1)*

We see this in the following scriptures; "Jesus said to them, 'If God were your Father, you would love me, for I came from God and now am here. I have not come on my own; but He sent me...'" *(John 8:42)* "Because of this, God in his wisdom said, 'I will send them prophets and apostles, some of whom they will kill and others they will persecute'" *(Luke 11:49)*. "Again Jesus said, 'Peace be with you! As the Father has sent me, I am sending you'" *(John 20:21)*.

Therefore an "apostle" is not someone who is sent by men or appointed by men, but by God. Again we go straight to scripture in order to see this, "Paul, an apostle - sent not from men nor by man, but by Jesus Christ and God the Father, who raised him from the dead..." *(Galatians 1:1)* "Paul called to be an apostle of Christ Jesus by the will of God..." *(1 Corinthians 1:1)* "He who receives you receives me, and he who receives me receives the one who sent me..." *(Matthew 10:40 - see also Acts 14:14; 15:23; Romans 16:7; 2 Corinthians 8:23; 1 Thessalonians 1:1)*

Increasing Apostolic Revelation

Now before I go any further, let me add to this by taking an excerpt from one of Ulf Ekman's books called, **"The Apostolic Ministry."**

"Apostles and prophets lay the foundation for the church: This century has seen increasing revelation on the ministry gifts. We have begun to understand what a pastor is, how an evangelist functions and what a teacher does. However, there are two special gifts that we need to understand so that God can develop strong local churches in the Last Days.

There is a fierce struggle concerning these gifts going on right now across the earth. The devil hates strong churches. He tries to crush them, tear them down and render them passive and ineffective. If he can remove the gifts that develop strong local churches, then he'll be satisfied. Apostles and prophets are the gifts that do this more than any other.

The apostle and the prophet are like spearheads, and the church is built on the foundation they lay (Ephesians 2:20). If they are not allowed to lay a proper foundation, then the church will lose direction, strength, anointing and spiritual insight. You can have good meetings, interesting conferences and fantastic campaigns without these gifts. But when the preachers leave and the crowds disappear, where is the strength that's needed for the local church? If you look closely, you'll see that the church is small, exhausted, confused and unsure of its direction.

The apostle and the prophet, especially the apostle, channel strength to the churches that helps them grow on a daily basis. **Churches are not built on conferences, campaigns and seminars. They are built by the steady labour of ordinary people, who are constantly developing and maturing.** Maturity, in a biblical sense, refers to increased vigour and stability, which makes us stronger. The apostle's ministry is vital and the bible gives us many examples of this" (Ekman 20-21).

Balanced Concept

Therefore it is important that we have a balanced concept of what an apostle is and what an apostle is really sent to do. Otherwise *(and just as I have witnessed around the world)*, this authentic and much needed role of the apostle is "misunderstood" and is desperately "lacking" within the church.

Often it is misconstrued as something intolerable, domineering and threatening. However in reality it couldn't be further from the truth and totally robs the church of a vital element that will help it to grow strong and STAY strong! So instead of complaining about all the weaknesses in the church we must allow the apostles to take back their rightful position in the body of Christ. Only then can we witness the kind of power, strength, authority and single-mindedness of the early church that we all crave to see.

I agree with Apostle Doctor Christian Harfouche; he says, "We believe in the pure unchanged, first century doctrine of Jesus Christ, as delivered by Jesus to His Body the Church by His servants, the Apostles, affirmed by the fathers and doctors, and agreed upon by the whole Church."

He go's on to say,

> "If there is anything that the world needs today, it is to see the Church living and walking in the power of the first-century faith."

The devil fears this kind of strength and will do anything to uphold the myth that apostles *(and prophets)* are obsolete and no longer necessary. The devil IS a liar! Oh how we need the apostolic ministry today and how little will be achieved without it.

Spiritual Puff Pastry

However in order for the church to be of significance once again, we need the apostolic ministry to do what it was sent *forth* to do. To bring: stability, maturity and growth.

None of us want to create works that have no substance. Puff pastry looks substantial on the outside but once you break through its veneer and crust there is no substance underneath! It looks impressive and glazed sitting up top but has little *(if any)* foundation. Spiritual puff pastry is a far cry from what God has planned for His church and for that which Christ died.

Resurrection Apostles

Now let's differentiate between the following types of apostles: **the resurrection and ascension apostles.** The original twelve *(minus Judas)* make up the first group, as they were directly commissioned by Jesus and received the inbreathing of resurrection life directly from Him, *(as the first fruits of His new creation).*

From Jesus they received proof of His being alive and the principles of His kingdom first hand. And once reinforced by Matthias *(Acts 1:12f)* they received the promised Holy Spirit at Pentecost. They are also known as the **APOSTLES OF THE LAMB.** "The wall of the city had twelve foundations, and on them were the names of the twelve apostles of the Lamb" *(Revelations 21:14).*

Furthermore Paul must be included in this particular group of apostles for the reason we see here, **"...and last of all he appeared to me also, as one abnormally born"** *(1 Corinthians 15:8).* And it is the testimony of this exclusive group of men that forms the definitive standard of teaching and doctrine for us. For example, we believe Jesus through *their* word, in the context of what Jesus spoke here in John

17:20, **"My prayer is not for them alone, I pray also for those who will believe in me through their message..."**

Strictly speaking *(concerning "resurrection apostles")* their only true successor is the New Testament itself; which preserves the record of their inspired testimony.

> *I have much more to say to you, more than you can now bear. But when he, the Spirit of truth, comes; he will guide you into all truth. He will not speak on His own; he will speak only what he hears, and he will tell you what is yet to come. He will bring glory to me by taking from what is mine and making it known to you...*
>
> (John 16:12-14)

All subsequent apostolic ministries *("ascension apostles")* must *submit to* and *accurately reflect* their testimony. It can be said like this; the words of the "resurrection apostles" are still primary and still scripture; but however, any other apostolic word is only *derivative (non-scripture).*

Unfortunately this is just where some of our modern-day apostles *(recent-past and present)* have made their errors. Some of them have wrongly imagined that this status of being an "apostle" gave their own words the same footing and weight as scripture itself! Clearly mistaken they have misunderstood their proper boundaries.

No Additional Revelation

To be clear about this, no one today is receiving any "additional revelation" that can add or take away from the original foundation of the gospel. We already have the revelation of the New Testament. Paul said, **"But though we, or an angel from heaven, preach any other gospel unto you than that, which we have preached unto you, let him be accursed"** *(Galatians 1:8 KJV)*. Paul warned that we are to take heed how we build upon the foundation that has already been laid *(1 Corinthians 3:10)*. Quite simply we can't add to it or take *anything* away from it.

Ascension Apostles

As mentioned already above, there exists a clear distinction between these two sets of apostles, those of the resurrection *(apostles of the Lamb)* and those of the ascension. In addition to this fact and to further explain this, it can be said that Paul was very much a "pivot" in that he was not only the last of the resurrection apostles *(who actually saw the risen Lord Jesus Christ)* but was also the first of a new series of apostles, called the **ascension apostles.**

To appreciate another *(ascension)* apostle, I turn again to the writings of Ulf Ekman and insert a paragraph from his book: **"The Apostolic Ministry - Can the Church Live Without It?"**

"The Apostolic Ministry has long-term effects: we must be set free from the idea of a religious 'St Paul' as portrayed in marble statues, icons and ancient historical images. We must see him in the unique role he had. It was Paul who received the revelation of Jesus' resurrection and wrote one-third of the New Testament. He remains the most important example of a Christian today after Jesus - our primary example.

Paul is an example in two areas: first he shows us how a Christian should live... lives of consistency. Second, he exemplifies the ministry of an apostle. He demonstrates the function of an apostle and the results that follow... Every ministry gift operates within the restrictions of time. The ministry of John the Baptist was effective for only a short period of time, yet his influence was great. Paul not only affected his era, but his influence has remained from generation to generation up to our present day.

An examination of the apostolic ministry will show that its influence continues even after the apostle has died. History speaks of men who weren't called apostles but were in fact just that. Wycliffe was definitely an apostle, as his degree of influence demonstrates. Huss, Luther, Calvin, Knox and Wesley were also apostles. How do we know? From their preaching, their message, their ministry and the enduring legacy they left behind. These are some of the signs of the apostle" (Ekman 23).

Yes! The apostle is certainly in it for *long haul* and not even his natural death can limit his influence. That's exciting! But there is much more to an apostle than this, we have only discussed some of the signs of an apostle - there is more.

In closing this particular chapter let me summarize by clearly saying, that not all apostles were like Paul. Some had lesser and some greater anointing, including different gifting. But the fact remains; there are two distinct categories of apostles: those of the resurrection and those of the ascension. Today apostles are still *commissioned* and *sent-forth,* and still possess great influence. Even today we can refer to them as **ascension apostles.**

❖

CHAPTER 10

Marks of an Apostle

In our last chapter we defined the difference between resurrection and ascension apostles. We looked at the basic meaning of the word apostle as being "sent-forth" by God. In this chapter we proceed by discussing the major *functions* and *characteristics* of an apostle.

> *The things that mark an apostle - signs, wonders and miracles - were done among you with great perseverance.*
> *(2 Corinthians 12:12)*

There are clear elements that dominate the calling and gifting of an apostle; which causes all apostles to act in similar ways. In other words, they can be very different in personality and background, but their gifting will have similar functions and boundaries.

Firstly and arguably the most important is that apostles are very good at *working-together,* whereas other gifts are more prone to being *competitive!* Although a true apostle will not build on the foundation of another *(usurp),* he will always allow other apostles to work together *with* him, in the spirit of relationship and collaboration.

In fact I would say that this is one of the *quickest* ways of detecting whether someone is an authentic apostle or not! **True apostles will work together.** Those who compete and clamber over others to "get-ahead," are ruthless like businessmen, *not* apostles.

Apostles do NOT Compete

Instead they have a unique understanding about foundations and just how *counter-productive* it can be to build upon the foundation that another has laid, and to usurp the authority of another. He will not waste his time. He would rather work in *conjunction with* or go somewhere else and lay down a whole new foundation!

Another feature or characteristic of the apostle is that of a PIONEER. They go first. When scripture said, **"...first apostles"** in 1 Corinthians 12:28, this was *not* just a sentiment of hierarchy but literally meant that apostles would *go-first, in front and pioneer!*

They break-open new ground and are not at all shy of ploughing where it has never been ploughed before. Nor do they shy away from *hard work.* **In fact you have never known real hard work until you have been around a true apostle** *(ask those who know!)* Their work ethic is second to none and they have *durability* and *spiritual backbone* that others even half their age can lack!

Their ability to endure hardship is another trait of the apostle. They are not fragile or delicate in their approach; they can be tough at times, yet remain loving and fatherly. They will observe and watch maturely, while others race and chase opportunities. They possess unequalled wisdom with a *panoramic scope* of view that keeps track on the pulse of where everything's up to, in the overall development of things!

This is unique to the apostle, whose spiritual scope and sight is much more *far reaching* than the other gifts of the body. Even though the prophet is considered the "seer," it is the role of the apostle to over-see the wider production and development of God's kingdom. This is why the prophet and apostle need each other and must work closely together - including the other gifts.

Apostles can have different gift mixtures, such as an apostle who is a pastor or an apostle who is a teacher and so forth. Still, regardless of gifting, we see during many different instances throughout scripture, how the apostles would work *together.*

One example for this is found in Acts 2:42 where it says; **"They devoted themselves to the _apostles'_ teaching... to the breaking of bread and to prayer."** Notice how the plural was used - **"apostle-s"** - showing that more than one apostle was involved in teaching those people.

No Fame-Game

Authentic apostles do not get caught up with the fame-game. In fact they are not driven by the need for fame, rather their need for **accomplishment!** Apostles are productive wherever they are, just as Paul was never found *stifled* by circumstance. Even when left to languish in prison for a season or under house arrest, Paul wrote some of his best works during those specific periods. **Nothing deterred him from his mission and nothing could chain down his revelation.** In fact hardship helped propel it!

In addition to all of this, apostles are not generally nervous about money - the abundance or lack of it! Scripture shows that Paul was very robust, knowing how to abase or abound. Whatever the situation *(or season)* called for, he was willing. And not just for the sake of proving how robust he could be, but for the furtherance of the gospel and advancement of the cause.

The Life of Preparation

So apostles are ready for just about anything and regular variations of season do not shake them, they just live prepared. All of which is another characteristic of an apostle. Apart from being extremely hard working and focused, they have a deep appreciation for "PREPARATION." They are always preparing, which is why they are always prepared. THEY LIVE PREPARED!

An apostle who does not feel *prepared* is generally not a happy apostle. This is when he can get a little gruff! It is also why you will never find an apostle sitting around doing nothing *(even in his sleep he is building or preparing **something!**)*

Sturdy is equal to "nerdy" in the world's eyes, but for an apostle **spiritual-backbone** is everything. One of their greatest satisfactions is derived from seeing "spiritual-maturity" outworked in the people. To help people *realize* and *release* the gifting that is within them.

In short, an apostle will always stir up the saints for ACTION and bring an explosion of life and activity wherever they are. *(Whether it's a good or bad reaction that's stirred, there's **always** a re-action around an apostle).*

So being lazy is a luxury around an apostle! No one gets away with it! They are hard wired to motivate people and therefore no one feels comfortable doing *nothing* around them! *(They can make even a hardened and self-confessed workaholic feel lazy!)*

However, it's all taken in their stride, by the inspiration of the Holy Spirit and each apostle possesses a specific *time-frame* to work in. They are uniquely aware of "time" and hate to waste it, working tirelessly to achieve the goals set before them.

*(Note: seasoned apostles don't tire with age because they have grown in wisdom and therefore also in their ability to **delegate** - most apostles could put an army to work, quite easily!)*

Spiritual Carelessness

Nothing displeases them more than to see rampant apostasy amongst God's people and spiritual carelessness or sloppiness. Therefore it's also good to point out that the apostle is not heavily prone to taking spiritual short cuts. No architect would do it. The safety of their overall structure would be compromised and the apostle sees things much the same way!

Another characteristic is ORDER; the apostle has an affinity with all-things-order. They generally bring order into chaos and restoration where there is brokenness. They are the ones trusted with God's blue print, as they are God's builders. Likewise, just as Nehemiah discovered he must remove the rubbish-heap before he could proceed building the walls of Jerusalem, an apostle will equally deal with the chaos that tries to hinder God's plan *(Nehemiah 1-3).*

In fact no other gift can maintain the level of order that an apostle can effectuate *(put into force or operation).* By his powers of delegation and skills of origination, he deals with any chaos *(naturally or spiritually speaking)* within his given sphere of influence and looks to permanently remove any obstacles that threaten to hinder or delay the successful completion of God's design.

Eight points to remember:

- **Plurality - apostles work as part of a team** *(1 Thessalonians 1:1; 2:6).* Let's look a little deeper at the apostle's ability to work alone but also as part of a team. He is not easily threatened and likes to work with others. In fact over "twenty men," at one time or another, were associated with Paul in his apostolic travels. **True apostles are not charismatic lone-**

rangers who lack and even despise the checks and balances of plurality. This is one reason that they like to bring on younger men in their calling in God, such as Paul did with Timothy.

- **Gifts and anointing** *(1 Thessalonians 1:5a)*. They have spiritual "power" not just ecclesiastical "status." **They enjoy the charisma of the Holy Spirit rather than their ordination papers** or may not even be officially ordained by a denomination.

  God is rising up a new breed of apostolic ministers who will readily admit that they are embryonic and earnestly desire and covet the wonders and miracles that are one of the signs of a true apostle. **"The things that mark an apostle - signs, wonders and miracles - were done among you with great perseverance"** *(2 Corinthians 12:12)*.

- **Has a proven character** *(1 Thessalonians 1:5b)*. We see in scripture that the apostles were men of integrity with mastery over wrong motives. For example they were not out to deceive, flatter or make money from those they ministered to *(1 Thessalonians 2:2-6)*, men worthy of imitating.

- **Is a man of patience and gentleness** *(1 Thessalonians 2:6-7)*. Because he is a man of faith he can afford to wait. Because he is a man of love he does not have to throw his weight about. **Building with living bricks takes time and trouble.** Taking another look at the sign of a true apostle, *(2 Corinthians 12:12)* we find the word **perseverance** *(patience KJV)*.

This reveals that true apostles are not mere remote office managers presiding over some new charismatic empire, which they lay claim to "covering." True apostles are prepared to spend time with individuals and not *just* leaders at that *(unless one is called to leaders specifically)*. They are *"on-site"* superintendents of the work.

- **A bearer of God's word** *(1 Thessalonians 2: 13)*. "And for this purpose I was appointed a herald and an apostle - I am telling the truth, I am not lying - and a teacher of the true faith to the Gentiles" *(1 Timothy 2:7)*. No man can ultimately be recognised as an apostle, who does not have a proven ministry as a preacher and a teacher of the word of God, for it is that which is the root of his authority, the source of his life and the dynamic of his ministry, he is a preacher and teacher of the word *before* he is an apostle.

- **He stands or falls by the church** *(1 Thessalonians 1:6-7)*. Like Peter, he should have been a fellow-elder in a local body. There, he can be tested and checked as he learns like everybody else, what it is to submit to one another in the fear of the Lord. As a local elder, he knows the responsibility of rule and pastoral care, which leaders in the church have, and then as an apostle, will be able to speak into other churches with greater sensitivity.

*To the elders among you, I appeal as a fellow-elder, a witness to Christ's sufferings and one who also will share in the glory to be revealed: Be shepherds of God's flock that is under your care, **serving** as overseers - not because you* *must, but because you are willing, as God wants you to be; not greedy for money, but eager to serve...*

(1 Peter 5:1-2)

- **One who is "sent-out" by the church to which he belongs,** an apostle carries credibility with him. Those who receive him can expect that he will have worked out *(learnt)* at home whatever he is laying on them as counsel; in this way Paul and Barnabas were "released" by the church at Antioch *(Acts 13:1-3)*.

Being sent out by the church of which they were a part - they are eager to return to give their support and report.

From Attalia they sailed back to Antioch, where they had been committed to the grace of God for the work they had now completed. On arriving there, they gathered the church together and reported all that God had done through them and how he had opened the door of faith to the Gentiles.

(Acts 14:26-27)

- **Finally and most importantly true apostles appreciate being "accountable."** This gives them a sense of security, saves them from the wrong kind of independence and reminds them they exist to serve the body and not themselves. They desire the best for the church *(1 Thessalonians 2:19)*.

❖

CHAPTER 11

Apostles Today?

Much of what is in this current book, "The Age of Apostolic Apostleship," has been taken from my articles called, "Truth for the Journey." Many across the Internet enjoy these articles; likewise we enjoy the tremendous feedback and positive responses they provoke!

In particular, an apostle who lives in Spain called, "Emilio Sevilla" dropped me a line to encourage but also to elaborate a little deeper on the meaning of the word apostle.

I quote him: "The word apostle means *'sent-to-establish'* because the word is made up of two words which are, *APO-STELLO - APO* means to be sent forth and *STELLO* means to establish... this is why apostles should not rest until they have established the kingdom in their given area..." End quote.

To see this in its various forms, we simply go to the Strong's Greek Concordance. To do so we take the precise place in scripture where Paul emphatically introduces himself as an "apostle" in his letter to the Corinthians, "Paul, called **to be** an apostle of Jesus Christ through the will of God..." *(1 Corinthians 1:1 KJV)* or as the Young's Literal Translation puts it, "Paul, a called *apostle* of Jesus Christ..."

The Greek word that was used here is the compound word apostolos *(ap-os'-tol-os, #G00652)* specifically meaning a delegate; specially, an ambassador of the gospel; officially a commissioner of Christ *("apostle") (with miraculous powers):* - apostle, messenger, **he that is sent.** However there are actually numerous compound words that help make up or have influence upon the meaning of this word apostle - which we have all become familiar with.

An Indispensable Ministry

For sure, the more we see what apostles do, the more we realize how indispensable their ministry is. The Acts of the Apostles is a book with no ending, as it records that which Jesus began to do and teach; He continues to do and say through His apostles, apostolic men or women who have the ability to father the church, its pastors and people. They are blessings from God, so much needed for today.

Yet there are still those who ask, **"are there apostles for today?"** Of course the answer has to be an unequivocal "Yes!" But let us qualify this answer because there are many who would answer, "No." To those who still question the validity of apostleship for today I would say that if there are prophets, evangelists, pastors and teachers then there must be apostles too.

Why? Because Jesus Himself gave and commissioned **all five** of these gifts to His bride and as long as this institution that we call church remains upon the earth - until Christ returns for it - then these five gifts will remain in full!

As stated before, apostles willingly work together just as the twelve did in the beginning, to lay the foundation for the very first church in Jerusalem. However were they really "unique" as some like to suggest, in an attempt to imply that apostles had their rightful place in the beginning, but are *obsolete* for today.

"Unique?" Yes, in the context that only they walked with Christ from the time of His baptism by John the Baptist, until He rose from the dead. They were also eyewitnesses of all that Jesus said and did. Some of them even recorded what they experienced *(testimony)*, which became part of the New Testament that we have and love today. In addition they not only received divine revelation, but also communicated that revelation *once and for all*. Yet even with this fact in place, the bible *never* stipulated that these were the first and final *(only)* apostles for the church.

Outside of the Original Twelve!

The most prominent apostles of all were Peter and Paul and arguably that the most important was Paul - who was not even among the original twelve, yet neither was Barnabas who we also found being called an apostle in scripture *(see Acts 14:14-15)*. This is the point. Scripture clearly states that they were both apostles. Furthermore, we find in Galatians 1:19 that James the brother of Jesus was also considered an "apostle."

In addition to this we find Paul writing about the apostolic ministry of Silvanus and Timothy *(who incidentally were also not part of the original twelve)* in his letter to the Philippians and there exists many more examples of this in scripture. So it appears there were indeed many more apostles that the bible identifies - outside of the original twelve!

They even lived and functioned during the same lifetime as the original twelve but were not included into that band. This identifies that the apostolic ministry was in circulation and was not limited to a certain number.

So the purpose of the apostles for the early church was clear. They helped lay the foundations and continued to establish and build upon what Christ had said and done. With this in mind then, let us ask the following question regarding today's church:

- Is the building finished?
- Is the bride ready?
- Is the church full-grown and are the saints completely equipped?
- Has the church attained its ordained maturity and unity?

I dare say this: only when the answer to these few questions is a **"YES,"** can we dispense with the apostolic ministry.

❖

CHAPTER 12

The Apostolic Ministry Functions Today

So we are slowly establishing the fact, using scripture to qualify, that the apostolic ministry was indeed something that Christ ordained Himself and is still in function today.

For the same God who worked through Peter as the apostle to the Jews also worked through me as the apostle to the Gentiles.
(Galatians 2:8 NLT)

Now in order for such apostolic ministry to function correctly and be at it's best *(as God intended and not as man-made hierarchy prefers it)*, we must be "in-charge-of-our-egos" especially where clerical *titles* are concerned! Even though Christ Himself gave such gifts their titles, we must not think of ourselves more highly than we aught *(Romans 12:3).*

A Government of Liberty

Rick Joyner says, "Church government under the original apostles was so unique, free, and effective that it defied definition. It was such a radical departure from anything the world had ever seen that it was impossible for the world to understand using any authority structure that was known. Like the other great principles of the faith, when there is an attempt to overly define it, the essence of what it is intended to be is often lost.

The first-century church government was not dependent on just one form, but on the anointing of the leaders who held the positions. Because of this, it had to be defined by the ones leading more than the system itself.

The apostles did not have a constitution, which decreed that they could dictate policy. Their authority came from something much higher—they had been with Jesus, and they were anointed by Him. Therefore, the only ones who could recognize their authority had to know the Lord and know the anointing.

The exercise of authority in the first-century church was both hierarchical and democratic. The main function of the apostles was to lay a solid foundation of doctrine and to establish a church government, which promoted liberty, not conformity. They accomplished this for a time. The freedom this allowed enabled the hearts of men to be converted by the power of truth and the conviction of the Holy Spirit - they were not converted by coercion.

From the beginning, this was intended to be the mode of operation for the spiritual authority exercised in the church. There was room for discipline and correction, but the ultimate penalty that the authorities of the church could exercise was the removal of the offender from fellowship until there was repentance.

The adherence of the apostles to this course of leadership was in such contrast to anything that had been known before, and certainly to the culture of the times, that it constituted the most extraordinary leadership ever exercised by any government at any time. As the church drifted from the genius of this extraordinary style of leadership, oppression grew, and the power of truth was replaced with a terrible, barbaric force intended to compel men to bend their knees to the dictates of church leaders without first bending their hearts to the truth" (Joyner 92-93).

First a Servant

Consider that in addition to holding-office, the apostle is also a ministry-gift to the body; nevertheless he is first a **SERVANT,** as are all the other gifts/offices that Christ ordained.

> It is the apostles who are assigned to take what the Spirit is saying to the churches and implement it by developing a strategy for moving forward.
>
> **Peter Wagner**

It is undeniable that Satan will try and destroy the anointed "structure" that God is restoring through His apostolic ministries. Satan knows full well that a house in division against itself *(against its own ordained structure)* will collapse. He capitalizes on this by triggering some of the "in-fighting" that exists between the different "gifts" in the body, *(making them totally counter-productive)*.

Individual gifts are deceived very effectively when simply steered down wrong paths *(that are not ordained for them)*. Let's be honest, a little "steering" here and there, is all it takes to make even the most "sincere" amongst us, totally ineffective! In other words our adversary might not be able to influence our love for Christ or dampen our zeal but he certainly can and does influence our egos, time and time again!

All apostolic ministries must never forget that they have been called to serve the church and not their own egos! Whenever power is involved, this can prove challenging *(1 Peter 5:5-8)*.

It's important to look at the apostle in relation to the other apostolic gifts. By way of a simple illustration, take the hand and imagine each of the fingers to represent one of the five fold ministry gifts that Christ gave to His body.

- **The index finger:** represents the prophet - the one who points the way and says just like Isaiah "This is the way; walk in it..." *(30:21)* Therefore he gives direction, tells of the spiritual condition of the church and exposes its sin!

- **The middle finger:** represents the evangelist. His ministry is more widespread than others. He reaches further. He is stifled if left in the confines of the church. He loves to be out in the field. He needs to be let loose to do his job, supported and equipped by the church that sends him out - to go beyond its confines and be effective.

- **The ring finger:** represents the pastor's ministry. He is totally committed to his flock - loving as a shepherd would - caring, encouraging and meeting the individual needs of his sheep.

- **The little finger:** represents the teacher's ministry - the finger small enough to clear away the wax in the ears so that folks can hear well and understand better!

- **Lastly the thumb:** represents the apostle. It is sturdier than the other fingers and can touch all of the others with ease! This implies that an apostle can function in all of the other ministry gifts - when necessary. He brings stability and flexibility, which is essential for the body to grow with strength and maturity.

However and perhaps most importantly is the fact that without a thumb it is impossible to "grasp" anything. **In fact only when the other fingers cooperate with the thumb - can the job get done!**

It's elementary then, that just as the fingers of one hand must work together, so too must apostolic ministries cooperate and collaborate together so that they can be of benefit to the body that they are called to.

Apostolic Gifts flowing Together

In his book, "Apostles, Prophets and the Coming Moves of God" Dr. Bill Hamon brings out the following:

"**Fivefold Ministries:** these are the fivefold ascension gift ministries as revealed in Ephesians 4:11 - apostle, prophet, evangelist, pastor and teacher. They are not gifts of the Holy Spirit per se, but an extension of Christ's headship ministry to the church. Their primary ministry and function are to teach, train, activate and mature the saints for the work of their ministries *(Ephesians 4:12-13)*.

Apostle: one of the fivefold ministries of Ephesians 4:11. The apostle is a foundation-laying ministry *(Ephesians 2:20)* that we see in the New Testament establishing new churches *(Paul's missionary journeys)*, correcting error by establishing proper order and structure *(first epistle to the Corinthians)*, and acting as an oversight ministry that fathers other ministries *(1 Corinthians 4:15; 2 Corinthians 11:28)*.

The New Testament apostle has a revelatory anointing *(Ephesians 3:5)*. Some major characteristics are **great patience** and manifestations of **signs, wonders and miracles.** We will know more and see greater manifestations concerning the apostle during the peak of the apostolic movement.

Prophet: he is a man of God whom Christ has given the ascension gift of a 'prophet' *(Ephesians 4:11; 1 Corinthians 12:28; 14:29; Acts 11:27; 13:1)*. A prophet is one of the fivefold ascension gift ministers who are an extension of Christ's ministry to the church. He is an anointed minister who has the gifted ability to perceive and to speak the specific mind of Christ to individuals, churches, businesses and nations.

Greek: 'prophetes' *(prof-ay-tace)* a foreteller, an inspired speaker *(Strong's Concordance, Vine's Concordance).* A proclaimer of a divine message, denoted among the Greeks as an interpreter of the oracles of gods.

In the Septuagint it is the translation of the word 'roeh' - a seer - indicating that the prophet was one who had immediate intercourse with God *(1 Samuel 9:9).* It also translates the word 'nabhi,' meaning either, *'one in whom the message from God springs forth, or one to whom anything is secretly communicated' (Amos 3:7; Ephesians 3:5).*

Prophetess: Greek 'prophetis' - the feminine of phrophet *(Gk. Prophetes).* A woman of God whom the Holy Spirit has given the divine prophetic ability to perceive and speak the mind of Christ on specific matters to particular people. Strong's - a *'female foreteller or an inspired woman.'* She is a specially called woman who functions like the New Testament prophet to minister to the body of Christ with inspired speaking and prophetic utterance *(Acts 2:17; 21:9; Luke 2:36; Isaiah 8:3; 2 Chronicles 34:22; Jude 4; Exodus 15:20).*

Prophetess is the proper title for a woman with this ascension gift and calling. **Prophet** is the proper title for a man with this ascension gift and calling.

Evangelist: the traditional view of the evangelist is a bearer of the *'Good News,'* proclaiming the gospel to the unbelieving world; exemplified by modern-day evangelists who preach the message of salvation in crusades and the like. However, Philip, the New Testament evangelist mentioned in Acts 21:8, demonstrated a strong supernatural dimension to the evangelistic ministry.

Philip preached the gospel to the lost *(Acts 8:5)*, moved in miracles *(8:6)*, delivered people from demons *(8:7)*, received instructions from an angel *(8:26)*, had revelation knowledge *(8:29)*, and was supernaturally translated from Gaza to Asotus *(8:26, 40)*. We are looking forward to the restoration of this type of prophetic evangelist to the body of Christ.

Pastor: Greek 'poiment' - a shepherd, one who tends, herds or flocks *(not merely one who feeds them)*, is used metaphorically of Christian pastors. Episkopeo *(overseer, bishop)* is an overseer, and Pesbuteros *(elder)* is another term for the same person as bishop or overseer. They normally give the title to the senior minister of the local church, regardless of his fivefold calling. It is a shepherding ministry to feed and care for the flock.

Responsibilities that appear connected with the pastoral ministry include oversight and care of the saints, providing spiritual food for their growth and development, leadership and guidance, and counsel. Prophetic pastors not only do the things normally associated with pastoring, but also move in supernatural graces and gifts of God *(prophesying, word of knowledge, healing)* and have the vision and willingness to develop the saints in their gifts and callings.

Teacher: an instructor of truth. *'All scripture is given by inspiration of God, and is profitable for doctrine, for reproof, for correction, for instruction in righteousness' (2 Timothy 3:16 KJV).*

A New Testament apostolic-prophetic teacher is one who not only teaches the letter of the word, but also ministers with divine life and Holy Spirit anointing *(2 Corinthians 3:6)*. He exhibits keen spiritual discernment and divine insight into the word of God and its personal application to believers.

Apostolic-Prophetic Lifestyle: these are the people who live their lives according to the logos and rhema word of God. The *logos* is their general standard for living and the rhema gives direction in specific areas of their lives. The fruit of the Holy Spirit is their characteristic motivation, and the gifts of the Spirit are their manifestation to meet the needs of mankind.

They are allowing their lives to become a prophetic expression of Galatians 2:20 *(KJV)*; *'I am crucified with Christ; nevertheless I live; yet not I, but Christ liveth in me: and the life which I now live in the flesh I live by the faith of the Son of God, who loved me, and gave Himself for me'"* (Hamon 279-281, 289).

The apostolic is in full swing. The best is yet to come. Much is being restored back to the church and we will see the power of the early church. The days of "Ananias and Sapphira" will return - where the fear of God will reign again and those outside the church walls will respect her position of authority on the earth.

There is power and authority when the apostolic ministry is allowed to function and flow by the Spirit of God, just as they were supposed to. I look forward with great expectation and anticipation to the complete restoration of all such things.

❖

Bibliography

- Cho, Paul Y. <u>More Than Numbers</u>. Copyright © 1984. Published by Word Publishing. Printed in UK.

- Ekman, Ulf. <u>The Apostolic Ministry</u>. Copyright © 1995. Published by Word of Life Publications. Printed in Sweden.

- Hamon, Bill. <u>Apostles, Prophets and the Coming Moves of God</u>. Copyright © 1997. Published by Destiny Image Publishers, Inc. Printed in USA.

- Joyner, Rick. <u>Shadows of Things to Come</u>. Copyright © 2001. Published by Thomas Nelson, Inc. Printed in USA.

- Maurer, Wilhelm. <u>Kirche und Synagoge</u>. ed. by Karl-Heinrich Rengstorf and Siegfried von Kortzfleisch. Copyright © 1968. Published by Ernst Klett Verlag. Printed in Germany.

- Strong, James. S.T.D., L.L.D. 1890. <u>Strong's Exhaustive Concordance; Dictionaries of the Hebrew and Greek Words</u>. e-Sword ® version 7.6.1 Copyright © 2000-2005. All Rights Reserved. Registered trade mark of Rick Meyers. Equipping Ministries Foundation. USA www.e-sword.net.

- Unless otherwise indicated, all scriptural quotations are from the HOLY BIBLE, NEW INTERNATIONAL VERSION ®. NIV ®. Copyright © 1973, 1978, 1984 by the International

❖

Ministry Profile

Doctor Alan Pateman, an apostle, is the President and Founder of **"Alan Pateman Ministries International"** (APMI), which was established in England back in 1987, a Christian-based *(parachurch)* non-profit and non-denominational outreach. This ministry is now focusing in two main areas: First **"Connecting for Excellence"** Apostolic Networking (CFE) and secondly, the teaching arm, **"LifeStyle International Christian University"** (LICU).

CFE is a multi-facetted missions organisation with the purpose of connecting leaders for divine opportunities and building lasting relationships, to touch the lives of leaders literally the world over. Apostle Dr Alan Pateman has to date ordained more than 500 ministers in over 50 NATIONS. In addition there are ministries, churches and schools who are in Association or Affiliation, looking to him for apostolic counsel and oversight.

Secondly LICU, which was founded in 2007, is a study program to help people discover their purpose and destiny. A global network of university campuses and correspondence students, demonstrating the Supernatural Kingdom of God through Doctrinal, Apostolic and Prophetic Teaching. Dr Alan holds the position of President/CEO, Professor of Theology, Biblical Studies and Apostolic Ministry. LICU is exploding throughout Europe, Asia and Africa, enhancing the Body of Christ

Dr Alan has authored more than 35 books including numerous teaching materials and LICU university courses (30) along with hundreds of Truth for the Journey articles on kingdom lifestyle *(that are regularly distributed globally via the internet).*

He is recognised as an Apostle, Bishop, Leadership Mentor, University Educator, Motivational Speaker, Connector and Author, who has also been featured on national and international TV and radio networks throughout the years.

Currently Apostle Alan, his wife Dr Jennifer reside in Lucca *(Tuscany)* Italy and travel out from their Apostolic Company.

- Alan Pateman Ph.D., D.Min., D.D., M.A., B.Th.

Academic Background

Dr. Alan Pateman attended several colleges throughout his training *(including studying Theology at Roffey Place, Horsham, UK and a Member of Kerygma - with Rev. Colin Urquhart and Dr. Bob Gordon - 1985-1987)* before being awarded a Doctorate of Divinity *(2006)* in recognition of his lifetime achievements by the International College of Excellence, now "DanEl Christian College" *(President: Dr. Robb Thompson USA)* also "Life Christian University" *(Dr. Douglas Wingate USA)* where he also earned a Bachelor of Theology B.Th. *(2006),* a Master of Arts in Theology M.A., a Doctor of Ministry in Theology D.Min., *(2007)* and Doctor of Philosophy in Theology Ph.D. *(2013)* from LICU.

❖

To Contact the Author

Please email:

Alan Pateman Ministries International

Email: apostledr@alanpateman.com
Web: www.AlanPatemanMinistries.com

*Please include your prayer requests
and comments when you write.*

❖

Other Books

Media, Spiritual Gateway

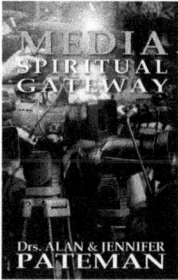

Let's face it; we live in the era of fake news! It's always existed, but never been quite so prominent. Today it's an all-out-war between fact and political fiction.

ISBN: 978-1-909132-54-2, Pages: 192,
Format: Paperback, Published: 2018
Also available in eBook format!

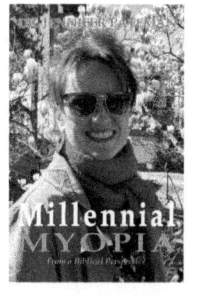

Millennial Myopia, From a Biblical Perspective

The standard for every generation is Jesus. However Millennial Myopia describes the trap of focusing everything on one particular generation or demographic cohort, at the exclusion and expense of all others. The Church cannot afford to make this mistake too.

ISBN: 978-1-909132-67-2, Pages: 216,
Format: Paperback, Published: 2017
Also available in eBook format!

Truth for the Journey Books

TONGUES, Our Supernatural Prayer Language

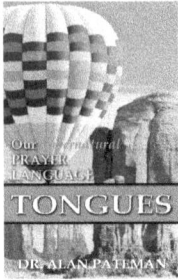

In writing to the church at Corinth, Paul encouraged them to continue the practice of speaking with other tongues in their worship of God and in their prayer lives as a means of spiritual edification. "He that speaketh in an unknown tongue edifies, charges, builds himself up like a battery."

ISBN: 978-1-909132-44-3, Pages: 144,
Format: Paperback, Published: 2016
Also available in eBook format!

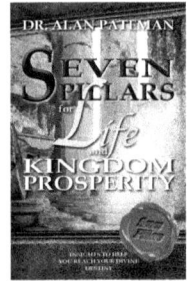

Seven Pillars for Life and Kingdom Prosperity

I submit these "Seven Pillars for Life and Kingdom Prosperity" to you, (Love, Prayer, Righteousness, Obedience, Connections, Management, Money). It's my desire that you walk in the triumphs that God has ordained for you.

ISBN: 978-1-909132-46-7, Pages: 220,
Format: Paperback, Published: 2016
Also available in eBook format!

Seduction & Control: Infiltrating Society & the Church

This book is a glance into the world of seduction and control, how they try to influence the Church through many powerful avenues such as the New Age, sexual education in our schools, basic entertainment; things that touch our everyday lives in order that we effectively and gradually become desensitised.

ISBN: 978-1-909132-00-9, Pages: 156
Format: Paperback, Published: 2015
Also available in eBook format!

Truth for the Journey Books

Kingdom Management for Anointed Prosperity

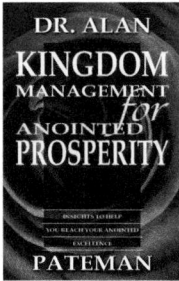

In his book, "Kingdom Management for Anointed Prosperity," Dr. Alan Pateman reveals how we can avoid living in continual crisis due to mismanagement. Life happens to all of us, but how we handle it matters most.

ISBN: 978-1-909132-34-4, Pages: 144,
Format: Paperback, Published: 2015
Also available in eBook format!

Why War: A Biblical Approach to the Armour of God and Spiritual Warfare

Spiritual warfare means different things to different people, but from a biblical standpoint Ephesians 6:10-18 gives us the best biblical definition of spiritual warfare possible. We can also see how God has thoroughly equipped us for victory not just self defence!

ISBN: 978-1-909132-39-9, Pages: 180,
Format: Paperback, Published: 2013
Also available in eBook format!

Forgiveness, The Key to Revival

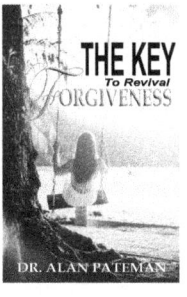

Scripture is absolute when it comes to forgiveness. IF we forgive, THEN we are forgiven. It's that simple but no one said it was easy! Nonetheless, forgiveness can be likened to a spiritual key that unlocks spiritual doors and opportunities!

ISBN: 978-1-909132-41-2, Pages: 124,
Format: Paperback, Published: 2013
Also available in eBook format!

Revival Fires - Anointed Generals Past & Present (Part Two of Four)

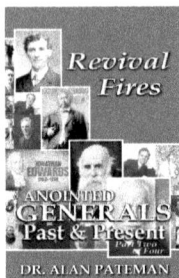

Seasons might be changing but God's Word remains the same. The heart of the author is to help train, equip and be a blessing to those men and women who will be willing to fulfil their potential in ministry and be properly equipped for service.

ISBN: 978-1-909132-36-8, Pages: 142, Format: Paperback, Published: 2012
Also available in eBook format!

Prayer, Touching the Heart of God (Part Two)

Touching the Heart of God is the very essence of prayer. Whether we are petitioning God with very specific requests or consecrating ourselves before Him and rededicating our lives - whatever the case may be – the true essence of all praying is "Touching the Heart of God."

ISBN: 978-1-909132-12-2, Pages: 180, Format: Paperback, Published: 2012
Also available in eBook format!

Prayer, Ingredients for Successful Intercession (Part One)

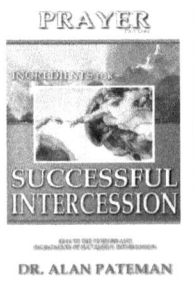

This Book is the first of two books on Prayer. Dr. Pateman provides an exhaustive study, showcasing the vital ingredients necessary for all successful prayer. An excellent power-packed teaching tool, either for the individual or for the local church prayer group, that's eager to lay a solid foundation but don't know where to start!

ISBN: 978-1-909132-11-5, Pages: 140, Format: Paperback, Published: 2012
Also available in eBook format!

Apostles: Can the Church Survive Without Them?

Before Jesus returns a significant increase of the anointing will be poured out on the Body of Christ, but can the Church handle such an anointing? *(Acts 5:5)* Billy Brim once said, "As much as the anointing is powerful to create, it is as powerfully destructive of evil." The fear of God will be restored with the apostolic and people will begin walking with such anointing, as we have never seen before!

ISBN: 978-1-909132-04-7, Pages: 164,
Format: Paperback, Published: 2012
Also available in eBook format!

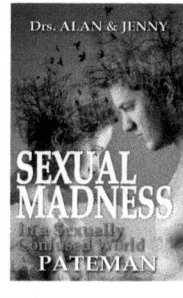

Sexual Madness: In a Sexually Confused World

This book discusses the sensitive subject of political correctness in our world today and the growing fear of causing offence in the public arena. It also discusses the rise of homosexuality, pedophilia and all other forms of sexuality, as there are many. Including modern statistics on pornography.

ISBN: 978-1-909132-02-3, Pages: 160,
Format: Paperback, Published: 2012
Also available in eBook format!

His Life is in the Blood

Blood is the trophy of every battle. The spilt blood of Jesus Christ is our trophy. It is our freedom from sin and bondage. Nothing can enter the blood-bought temples of the Holy Ghost! This book will encourage you to apply the blood of Jesus our Passover Lamb to your life, just as the children of Israel did in the Old Testament. Not merely talking or reading about it, but applying it.

ISBN: 978-1-909132-06-1, Pages: 152,
Format: Paperback, First Published: 2007
Also available in eBook format!

Truth for the Journey Books

WINNING by Mastering your Mind

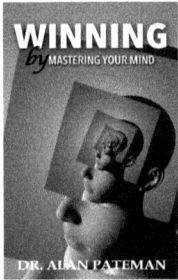

Someone once said, "Happiness begins between your ears and your mind is the drawing room for tomorrow's circumstances..." Remember, what happens in your mind will happen in time, and therefore one of our first priorities must be mind-management.

ISBN: 978-1-909132-40-5, Pages: 136, Format: Paperback, Published: 2017
Also available in eBook format!

Dear Friends,

Have you considered becoming one of our international students? We are privileged to welcome you, from around the world, to "LifeStyle International Christian University" *(the teaching arm of Alan Pateman Ministries International).* **An English speaking university** dedicated to your success; to see you trained and equipped to fully succeed in your God given Destiny.

It is our passion to raise up the leaders of tomorrow, who will have influence in all realms of authority, including the Body of Christ. Men and women of strategy, wisdom and true godliness, who'll stand with stature and maturity in this hour.

It's undeniable that in today's world, recognised education has become indispensable, therefore it is our desire to offer well balanced and well structured courses. Those that have been written by gifted and talented ministers of God, who seek to be inspired by God's Holy Spirit.

Consequently we have put together a **flexible curriculum,** designed both for correspondence students and campuses, which is a strategy to reach the distant learner; whether provincial, national or international. In fact we have many correspondence students from around the world, including a growing number of successful campuses, in various countries.

This is a growing platform, where men and women of dignity and passion, can grow and be established in their God given endeavours. As God is the healer of the nations, we pray and believe that many of our alumni will go on to **become world changers** in their own right.

We are proud of each and every one of our LICU students.

It would be our pleasure if you would join them on this incredible journey!

Doctor Alan Pateman

Alan Pateman Prof. Ph.D., D.Min., D.D., M.A., B.Th.
PRESIDENT AND CEO
www.licuuniversity.com www.cfeapostolicnetwork.com
Email: info@licuuniversity.com Mob: +39 366 329 1315

For more information visit our website/facebook or contact our office, using the details below:

Website: www.licuuniversity.com
Facebook: www.facebook.com/LICUMainCampus
Email: info@licuuniversity.com
Telephone: +39 366 329 1315

All Books Available

at

APMI PUBLICATIONS

Email: publications@alanpateman.com
*Also Available from Amazon.com
and other retail outlets.*

*If you purchased this book through Amazon.com
or other and enjoyed reading it, or perhaps one of
my other books, I would be grateful if you could
take a couple of minutes to write a Customer
Review, many thanks.*